Job Interview Questions Series 2020 Edition

ADVANCED JAVA

INTERVIEW QUESTIONS YOU'LL MOST LIKELY BE ASKED

372
Interview Questions

Advanced JAVA

Interview Questions You'll Most Likely Be Asked

ISBN-10: 1-946383-22-8
ISBN-13: 978-1-946383-22-8

Library of Congress Control Number: 2011907325

This publication is designed to provide accurate and authoritative information in regard to the subject matter covered. The author has made every effort in the preparation of this book to ensure the accuracy of the information. However, information in this book is sold without warranty either expressed or implied. The Author or the Publisher will not be liable for any damages caused or alleged to be caused either directly or indirectly by this book.

Vibrant Publishers books are available at special quantity discount for sales promotions, or for use in corporate training programs. For more information please write to **bulkorders@vibrantpublishers.com**

Please email feedback / corrections (technical, grammatical or spelling) to **spellerrors@vibrantpublishers.com**

To access the complete catalogue of Vibrant Publishers, visit **www.vibrantpublishers.com**

Table of Contents

Dear Reader,

Thank you for purchasing **Advanced JAVA Interview Questions You'll Most Likely Be Asked.** We are committed to publishing books that are content-rich, concise and approachable enabling more readers to read and make the fullest use of them. We hope this book provides the most enriching learning experience as you prepare for your interview.

Should you have any questions or suggestions, feel free to email us at reachus@vibrantpublishers.com

Thanks again for your purchase. Good luck with your interview!

- Vibrant Publishers Team

facebook.com/vibrantpublishers

Advanced Java Interview Questions

Review these typical interview questions and think about how you would answer them. Read the answers listed; you will find best possible answers along with strategies and suggestions.

www.vibrantpublishers.com

This page is intentionally left blank.

2: Differentiate between Externalizable and Serializable interfaces?

Answer:

Serializable interface is a marker interface so you don't have to override the methods in it. But you have to override the readExternal() and writeExternal() methods of the Externalizable interface.

When you implement the Serializable interface, the JVM takes care of file streaming which can be inefficient at times. But since you are overriding the streaming methods in Externalizable interface, it is a more efficient way to file streaming.

If you are not sure of how to perform the IO streaming efficiently for your application it is better to implement the Serializable interface. If you can efficiently perform IO streaming specific to your application, Externalizable interface implementation is the best way.

When all or most of the attributes of an object has to be serialized, implementing the Serializable interface with use of transient variable as required will be more efficient. But when you have to serialize some dynamic attributes of large Java objects with too many attributes, implementing the Externalizable interface is a better way as you can specify what all have to be serialised efficiently in the overridden methods.

3: What is a serialVersionUID? How is it used?

Answer:

A Serial Version UID is a unique identifier for a serializable class to make sure that the serialised and the deserialised object refers

Chapter 1

Object Serialization

1: What is Object Serialization? How is it done?

Answer:

Object Serialization is writing the object's properties and behaviour into a byte stream or a file. All the serializable objects referred inside it are also written into the file. This makes the object constant or invariable. This is usually used when an object has to be sent over a network. An object is Serializable when the class implements the Externalizable or Serializable interface. The object can then be passed on to the ObjectOutputStream which in turn passes it to the file output stream. When your object implements the Serializable interface which is a marker interface, you don't have to implement its methods whereas when the Externalizable interface is implemented you have to implement the readExternal() and writeExternal() methods.

to the same version. The Java compiler creates a unique serialVersionUID if it is not defined in the program. It is best to define a serialVersionUID for every serializable class as otherwise the JVM will not able to identify the class when its version changes. Everytime you change an attribute of the serializable class, the JVM creates a new serialVersionUID if it is not user-defined. So the best practice is to define a serialVersionUID for all serializable classes in Java so that the multiple versions will refer to the same object.

4: What is the next best option is we do not go for Object Serialization?

Answer:

Java uses Object Serialization to store the data permanently in the system's storage. The same can be done using other methods such as database, XML and JSON which is a comparatively recent method that uses Javascript. Using a database to store objects is a very common method. You can use the ORM or Object Relational Mapping to store and retrieve objects from and to the database. XML based data storage and transfer is now being commonly used by many web services. This is probably the most popular way to transfer data over the internet. The JSON data transfer is a relatively new format in use. Implementation of JSON is quite simple and it is integrated to most of the web browsers as it is based on Javascript.

5: How can the Java objects exist beyond the lifetime of the virtual machine?

Answer:

Object serialization allows Java objects to live beyond the lifetime of JVM.

6: I wish to serialize a collection. Is it a must to have all its members Serializable?

Answer:

Yes. All members of a collection or an array must be Serializable in order to Serialize it.

7: How to exclude certain variables from object's serialized state?

Answer:

To exclude variables from the process of serialization, they should be marked as transient.

Example: Transient private String variable;

8: Is it true to say that during object serialization class and instance variables that are not marked as transient are also serialized?

Answer:

No. Static variables belonging to the class are not saved as the part of serialized object. Also the transient class variables will not be part of serialized object.

9: What will happen if I try to serialize an object of a class that implements Serializable interface, but also includes a non-Serializable object?

Answer:

java.io.NotSerializableException will be thrown at runtime.

10: Once de-serialization is done, what values will transient variables get?

Answer:

Transient variables get default values after de-serialization.

11: You are making a class Serializable by implementing Serializable interface. Which methods are to be implemented?

Answer:

None.

12: Consider the following scenario:

public class ClassA extends ClassB implements Serializable{

ClassA extends from ClassB.

ClassA implements Serializable.

ClassA instance is serialized.

ClassA instance is de-serialized.

What values will the variables of ClassB get?

Answer:

ClassB's constructor will run and the variables will get the values assigned during the construction of the object.

13: What is the purpose of using serialVersionUID?

Answer:

serialVersionUID provides versioning system for every Serializable class. During de-serialization process, serialVersionUID provides means of checking whether data read from the input stream is compatible with the current class definition.

14: serialVersionUID is a static field declared in a Serializable class. Is it also serialized?

Answer:

serialVersionUID is a static field that is also serialized along with the other data. During de-serialization, the de-serialized serialVersionUID has to match to the serialVersionUID declared in the class definition.

15: What happens if serialVersionUID of de-serialized object does not match to the one declared in the class definition?

Answer:

java.io.InvalidClassException is thrown.

16: Consider that you have a Serializable class without serialVersionUID. How compiler will handle this?

Answer:

Java compiler adds serialVersionUID automatically and its value is based on the fields declared in the class.

17: What methods are there in Serializable interface?

Answer:

Serializable interface is a marker interface and has no methods. It simply tells the object serialization tools that the class is Serializable.

18: In which scenarios serialization should be used?

Answer:

Objects are serialized when sending over the network.

19: What can be the cause of NotSerializableException during object serialization?

Answer:

If a class is to be serialized, it has to implement Serializable interface. It is also important that all the objects included in that class are also Serializable. NotSerializableException is thrown if any of the included objects is not Serializable.

20: Which methods can be overridden to change default serialization behavior in order to control complex object serialization process?

Answer:

writeObject() and readObject() can be implemented to control complex object serialization process. By doing so, we can provide additional information to serialize and de-serialize objects.

21: Which interface is to be implemented if we want to have complete control over your class's serialization process?

Answer:

java.io.Externalizable interface is to be implemented.

22: Name the methods that are to be overridden when Externalizable is implemented.

Answer:

readExternal and writeExternal are to be overridden when Externalizable is implemented.

23: Consider the following scenario:
public class Parent implements Serializable

..

public class Child extends Parent

..

Is Child class Serializable?

Answer:

Child class inherits serialization from its object hierarchy and it is Serializable.

24: Is it correct to say that when an object is de-serialized, its constructor is called?

Answer:

De-serialization means restoring the serialized object and not re-constructing it. The constructor is not called in the de-serialization process.

25: I have a class called Student that is Serializable. It has an instance variable of type String called 'name'. Since 'name' is not of primitive type, should we expect serialization failure?

..

public class Student implements Serializable{
private String name;

..

Answer:

java.lang.String itself is Serializable, therefore Student class can be serialized.

26: Are all primitive wrapper classes Serializable?

Answer:

Yes. All primitive wrapper classes implement Serializable interface.

27: Assume you have a Serializable class where its super class does not implement Serializable interface. The super class defines a no- argument constructor and a String argument constructor. Which constructor of the super class will get called during de-serialization?

Answer:

No-argument constructor will get called. It should be accessible to the Serializable subclass class.

28: Consider the following scenario:

You have a Serializable class without serialVersionUID defined. You serialize it. You add a new instance variable in your Serializable class and de-serialize its already serialized instance. What will happen?

Answer:

Since serialVersionUID was not defined in the Serializable class, JVM will generate that. Once you add or remove instance variables in the Serializable class, the value of serialVersionUID will change. In the given scenario, java.io.InvalidClassException will be thrown.

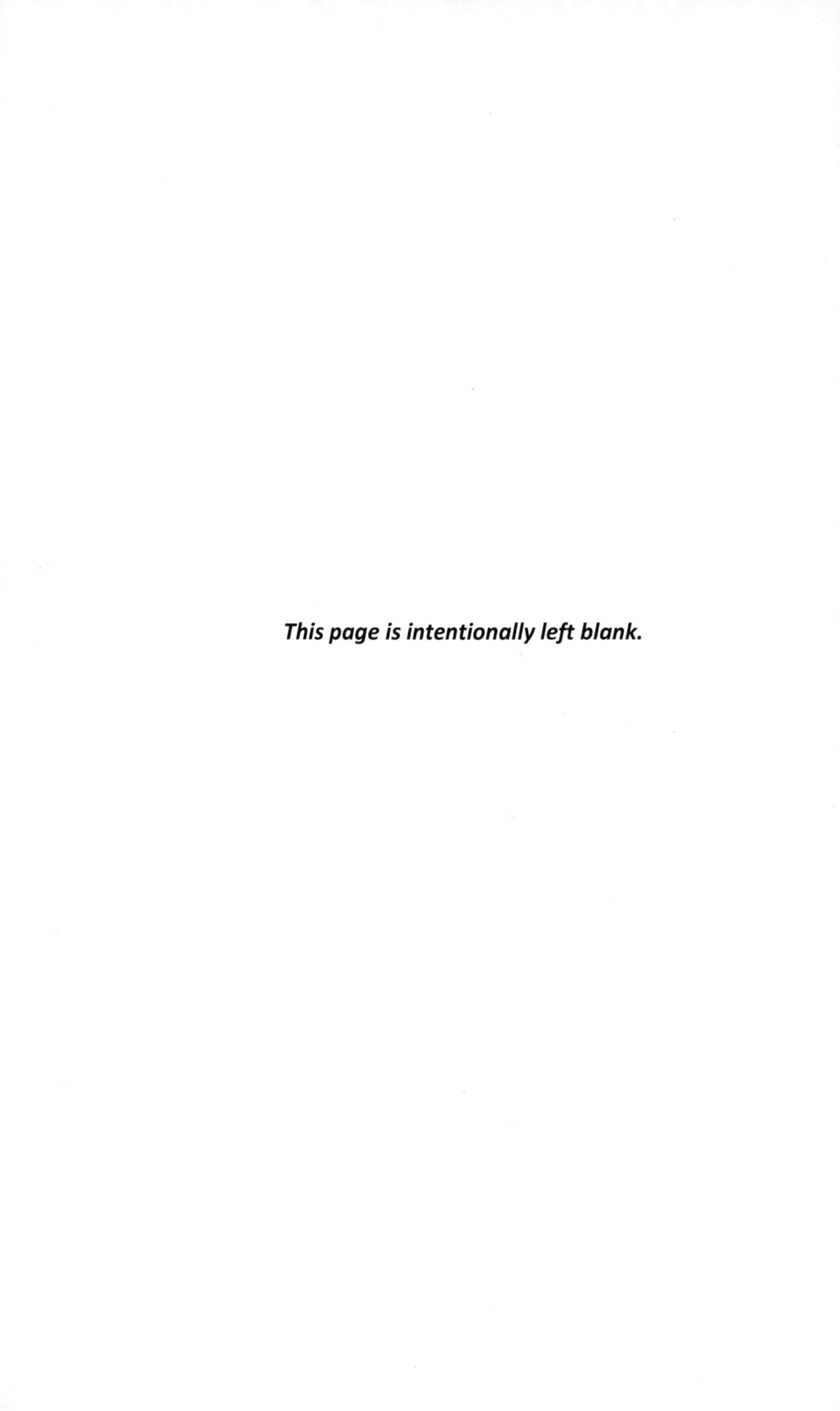

This page is intentionally left blank.

Chapter 2

Generics

29: Explain Java Generics.

Answer:

Java Generics allows creating collections that accept only specific type of data and thus you can eliminate type-casting. Another advantage of Generics is that you can create generic algorithms or methods that works for different data types without having to program separately for each data type.

Example:

```
List<String> listGen = new ArrayList<String>();  // We are declaring the ArrayList to store string objects

listGen.add("hello");  // adding a string

String strGen = listGen.get(0);  // Since the ArrayList was declared for string objects, no type-casting is required.
```

In the above code, if you add the following line, it will throw a compile time error:

listGen.add(21); // *compile time error as 21 is not a string*

30: Write a program to explain Generic Methods.

Answer:

```
public class exampleForGenericMethod{
    public static < E > void printArrayElements(E[] elementsVal) {
    for ( E elementVal : elementsVal){
        System.out.println(elementVal);
    }
    System.out.println();
        }
public static void main( String abcs[] ) {
    Integer[] myIntArray = { 15, 25, 35, 45, 55 };
    Character[] myCharArray = { 'H', 'E', 'L', 'L', 'O', 'W', 'O', 'R', 'L', 'D'
    };
    System.out.println( "The Integer Array is:" );
    printArrayElements (myIntArray  );
    System.out.println( "The Character Array is: " );
    printArrayElements ( myCharArray );
        }
        }
```

This program will print:

The Integer Array is:

15

25

35

45

55

The Character Array is:

H

E

L

L

O

W

O

R

L

D

We have used the same method and avoided method overloading also and instead used Java Generics.

31: Differentiate between List<? extends T> and List <? super T>

Answer:

The symbol ? represents a wildcard meaning any type. So *? extends T* means the list will accept any object which extends T or which is a sub-class of T. *? super T* means List will accept any object which is a super class of T. So List <? extends Number> will accept Integer type and Float types meaning List<Integer> and List<Float> will be fine. List <?> will mean that a list of any type can be created. List<?> means List<String> and List<Integer> are fine.

32: Explain the following code:

Case 1:

List listORTExample = new ArrayList(); // Line 1

```
listORTExample.add("abc"); // Line 2
listORTExample.add(123); // Line 3
String strItem = (String) listORTExample.get(0); // Line 4
strItem = (String) listORTExample.get(1); // Line 5
```

Case 2:

```
List<String> listOSExample = new ArrayList(); // Line 6
listOSExample.add("abcd"); // Line 7
listOSExample.add(1234); // Line 8
strItem = listOSExample.get(0); // Line 9
```

Answer:

Line 3 – Though the compiler will allow this a runtime exception will be thrown

Line 4 - Explicit cast is required as the List was not declared as String Type

Line 5 – Will throw ClassCastException because Integer cannot be cast in String

Line 8 – This line will throw a compiler error which is better than runtime Exception as against Line 3

Line 9 – Thanks to Line 6 where the Arraylist is declared for String Objects, no explicit casting is required

This is a classic example of how Java Generics improves the program.

33: Explain the Type Parameters in Generics.

Answer:

A Type Parameter is a place holder for argument types. Java has 5 type parameters

T denotes a Type

E denotes an Element

K denotes a Key

N denotes a Number

V denotes a Value

A Type parameter can be used for an argument and return type of methods, a target type in type-cast and an open type of argument for parameterized methods. A Type parameter cannot be used to create an object, array or in exception handling. It cannot be static and cannot be used with instanceOf operator. It cannot be used as a supertype or a class literal.

34: How to avoid casting when retrieving elements from a collection?

Answer:

Casting can be avoided using Generic collections.

Example:

```
List<String> gList = new ArrayList<String>();
```

35: Review the following code. Will it compile? Will it run?

```
public static void main(String[] args) {
List<String> typeSafeList = new ArrayList<String>();
typeSafeList.add(new String("string1"));
addElementsToList(typeSafeList);
String a = typeSafeList.get(1);
}
private static void addElementsToList(List list){
list.add(new Integer(10));
```

}

Answer:

The code will compile fine but will fail with the following exception:

java.lang.ClassCastException: java.lang.Integer cannot be cast to java.lang.String

36: Can you use more than one parameterized type in a declaration? Give an example.

Answer:

It is possible.

Example:

```
public class UseTwo<T, X> { }
```

37: How can you declare a generic method using a type say: T, which is not defined in the class?

Answer:

```
public <T> void makeList(T t) { }
```

The syntax is a bit tricky. This method has void as return type and declares the type before the return type.

38: Can you instantiate an array of a generic type?

Answer:

Generic arrays can be declared but cannot be instantiated just like a normal array. It gives a compile-time error since the type of the array is not known during compilation. Instead, it has to be instantiated using the new object() and type cast to an array. Another option is to create a parameterised array without mentioning the type. For example, the following code works:

```
arrType<String> [] abc = new arrType[50];
```

But this will not work:

```
arrType2<xyz> [] abc = new arrType<xyz>[50];
```

This page is intentionally left blank.

Chapter 3

CORBA

39: Explain CORBA and how it serves Java.

Answer:

CORBA or the Common Object Request Broker Architecture is a standard set by the OMG or Object Management Group to aid the communication between different systems having diverse platforms. CORBA is especially useful in a client-server or network architecture where the server has to interact with many devices having different operating systems and hardware structure. CORBA provides language and location transparency. CORBA uses the concept of a stub and skeleton to interact with various requests and objects. A stub is just like an object to the caller and will have access to the methods and attributes of the object. When a particular method of the object is called over a network, the stub passes on the information to the skeleton which in turn calls the method and passes on the result to the stub which is passed on to the network. CORBA is popular as it lets the applications based in Java and many other languages on the server to interact freely with the devices and applications on the client's device. CORBA can handle a large volume of data and there are specialised versions of CORBA running in real-time systems.

40: Explain the Life Cycle of CORBA application.

Answer:

The Life Cycle of CORBA applications involves 4 basic stages – First the CORBA application defines the service as interfaces in the IDL.

a) Then it compiles the IDL and generates the client stub and server skeletons.
b) It then implements the services and associates them with the skeletons by means of the POA or portable object adapter
c) Finally it publishes the service with a Trading or Naming Service to be used by the clients

And on the client side:

a) CORBA application contacts the Naming Service for the particular service and recovers the object reference.
b) It uses the IDL-compiler generated stubs to call upon operations on the object reference. Otherwise, clients can consult the IR or the Interface Repository to understand the operations supported by the service and then use the DII or the Dynamic Invocation Interface to dynamically create requests using the correct parameters.
c) It processes the incoming information or exceptions.

41: Explain CORBAservices and CORBAfacilities.

Answer:

The Object management Group or the OMG has numbered out some basic services which are generally required by most of the applications and included those in CORBAservices. Only the basic framework is provided and the implementation or process involved in these services has to be defined separately. The implementation of CORBAservices does not come with basic CORBA products and the CORBA vendors can provide different implementations depending on their CORBA products. Examples of CORBAservices are Event Service, Licensing Service, Naming Service etc. Depending on the CORBA product that a vendor is selling, they can define its functionality. CORBAfacilities are a handful of common processes or methods which are generally used by various applications. CORBAfacilities incude horizontal facilities like user interface, information processing etc. which are common to all types of applications and vertical facilities like general ledger and imagery which are specific to an industry. CORBAfacilities, especially the vertical facilities, have to be implemented explicitly by the CORBA product vendor. Some CORBAfacilities are intended to be used in specific domains only like imagery.

42: Explain how objects are passed in CORBA.

Answer:

Objects are usually passed by address or reference or by value. When an object is passed by reference, it always accesses the value at the address of the object and when the object's value changes, accordingly the referenced value also changes. This is the best way to access an object. When an object is passed by value, a copy of the object is created on the client and accessed. If the actual object's value changes, it does not affect the program as the object's copy is being accessed by it. In CORBA all objects are passed by reference only though CORBA is considering passing the objects by value also which may be included in the future versions or releases. This is because during remote method calls, the overhead is more as the program has to wait for the object to be released by the owner for accessing.

43: Which operation invocation techniques are provided by CORBA 2.0?

Answer:

The three operation invocation techniques provided by CORBA 2.0 are:

a) Synchronous
b) Deferred Synchronous and
c) One-way

44: What is Synchronous operation invocation technique?

Answer:

In Synchronous operation technique, the client invokes an operation. It then pauses in order to wait for a response.

45: What is the Deferred Synchronous operation invocation technique?

Answer:

In Deferred Synchronous operation invocation technique, the client invokes an operation and then continues processing. Later the client can poll or block waiting for a response.

46: What is the One-way operation invocation technique?

Answer:

In One-way operation invocation technique, the client invokes an operation and does not wait or expect any response in return. The ORB guarantees the request delivery.

47: How are the services offered by distributed object defined?

Answer:

Interface Definition Language defines the services offered by a particular distributed object.

48: Which CORBA service defines how objects are copied, moved, created and removed?

Answer:

Object life cycle service defines them.

49: Name the CORBA service that decouples the communication between distributed objects.

Answer:

Events service decouples the communication between distributed objects.

50: Does an object interface represent how it is or will be implemented?

Answer:

No. An object interface only indicates the supported operations.

51: Is it correct to say that IDL provides object's implementation?

Answer:

No. IDL provides the contract between code using the object and the code implementing the object. The actual implementation is done in programming language.

Example: Java, C++

52: Name the programming languages for which OMG has standardized on language bindings.

Answer:

OMG Object Model is suited for middleware as it defines the requests, objects, attributes, types, operations and exceptions used in the programs. Objective languages such as C, Java, COBOL, Ada, C++, Smalltalk, Lisp, and Objective C programming languages support OMG Object Model. The main disadvantage of OMG is that it does not support User Interfaces.

53: Name the IDL basic data types.

Answer:

IDL's basic data types are long, short, string, float.

54: You want to use constructed data types in IDL. What choices do you have?

Answer:

struct, union, enum, sequence

55: Which compiler is used to compile IDL declarations?

Answer:

IDL compiler

56: What is used by the client to issue a request on a CORBA object?

Answer:

Client uses an object reference to issue a request on a CORBA object.

57: IDL construct 'module' corresponds to which Java construct?

Answer:

package construct.

58: IDL construct 'operation' corresponds to which Java construct?

Answer:

method construct.

59: Which fundamental mechanisms are available to obtain object references?

Answer:

Object references can be obtained by passing it as a parameter, by returning it as result or by converting a string into an object reference. These are supported by ORB.

This page is intentionally left blank.

Chapter 4

Threading

60: Explain the different stages of a thread.

Answer:

Java Threads basically have 6 stages and they are:

a) **New** – when the thread has not yet started processing or running.
b) **Runnable** – when the thread is being executed in the JVM
c) **Blocked** – when the thread is blocked and is waiting for a monitor lock
d) **Waiting** – when the thread is waiting for an indefinite period for another thread for a particular process
e) **Timed_Waiting** – when the thread is waiting for a specified amount of time for a particular process
f) **Terminated** – when the thread has stopped or exited.

61: Explain the output of the following program.

```
public class myThreadTrial1 {
    private static class myDaemonThread1 extends Thread {
        public myDaemonThread1() {
            setDaemon(true);
        }
        @Override
        public void run() {
            try {
                Thread.sleep(1000);
            } catch (InterruptedException e) {
            }
        }
    }
    public static void main(String[] abcs) throws
    InterruptedException {
        Thread myThread1 = new myDaemonThread1();
        myThread1.start();
        myThread1.join();
        System.out.println(myThread1.isAlive());
    }
}
```

Answer:

The output is 'false'. Though myDaemonThread1 is a daemon thread as we have set it using setDaemon(true), when we call the method myThread1.join(); the main thread will wait till the daemon thread has finished executing. So later when we call myThread1.isAlive() it will no longer be alive.

62: Does the following code indicate a safe thread implementation?

```
public class DblChkSingleton {
    private DblChkSingleton instanceI = null;
    public DblChkSingleton getInstance() {
        if (instanceI == null) {
            synchronized (DblChkSingleton.class) {
                if (instanceI == null) {
                    instanceI = new DblChkSingleton ();
                }
            }
        }
        return instanceI;
    }
}
```

Answer:

This code is not thread-safe. Though it is synchronized and the instance is double checked, the JIT can always set the reference to the new instance of an object before its constructor is fully executed. So the getInstance() may return an object that is not fully initialized. This issue can be sorted out in Java 5 with the Volatile keyword. Volatile objects become visible to other objects only after its constructor has completed execution.

63: We know what a Deadlock is. Explain Livelock.

Answer:

A Livelock happens when 2 or more threads block each other because of another thread. Unlike the deadlock situation where the locked threads remain in the same state, in a livelock, the threads can change their state but still will remain locked. For example, 2 threads are trying to get 2 locks but release a lock which they already acquired when they are unable to get one of the locks. Now both the threads will try to lock the 1st thread at the same time. So if one thread T1 gets the first lock L1 and the second thread T2 gets the second lock L2. Since both T1 and T2 want both L1 and L2 they both release their locks and try again. So this situation will go on till one of the threads gets both the locks.

64: Explain with example how to create a thread.

Answer:

Threads can be created in 2 ways – by extending the Thread Class or by implementing the Runnable Interface. When you extend the Thread class, you have to override the run() method, create an instance of the subclass and invoke the start() method to execute the thread. When you implement the Runnable interface, you have to implement the run() method, create an instance of that class and pass on its reference to the thread constructor to start execution of the thread.

Code Example by extending the Thread class:

```
public class myNewThread extends Thread{
    public void run(){
        // here write the code to be executed when the thread runs
    }
    public static void main(String [] abcs){
        myNewThread mnt = new myNewThread();
        mnt.start();
```

```
    }
}
```

Code Example by implementing the Runnable interface:

```
public class myNewThread implements Runnable{
    public void run(){
        // here write the code to be executed when the thread runs
    }
    public static void main(String [] abcs){
        myNewThread mnt = new myNewThread ();
        Thread myThread = new Thread(mnt);
        myThread.start();
    }
}
```

65: Explain wait(), yield() and sleep() methods in Java.

Answer:

The wait() method is used to release the lock of an object a thread has put and it goes into a suspended state. It can be activated when a notify() or notifyAll() is called for the same object. The yield() method releases the lock of an object so that if any other thread is waiting for the same object, it can access the released object. The sleep() method will not release the object, it will only keep the object waiting for n milliseconds or till it is interrupted.

66: There are three threads Thread1, Thread2 and Thread3? How do you ensure sequence Thread1, Thread2, Thread3 in Java?

Answer:

The simplest method for sequencing in Java is by using the join()

method in the Thread class. So the code should be implemented such that Thread3 starts first, then call Thread2.join() and then call Thread1.join(). So Thread1 will start first, Thread2 will join when Thread1 finishes and Thread3 will start when Thread2 finishes. This is the easiest and simplest way to implement sequencing in threads. Always start the last thread first and then join the threads in the reverse order. It will be executed in the required order.

67: What are the two ways of creating Threads in Java?

Answer:

We can extend the Thread class and override public void run() method or we can call the Thread constructor that takes a Runnable argument.

68: What happens if start() is called more than once on same thread object?

Answer:

It will throw a RuntimeException.

69: Can you create more than one Thread objects using the same Runnable object as the target?

Answer:

No. It is illegal.

70: When does a thread object become a thread of execution?

Answer:

On invoking a Thread's start(), it becomes thread of execution.

71: When is a thread considered alive?

Answer:

A thread in execution state is considered alive.

72: A new thread is started. In which state it will enter?

Answer:

When a new thread has been created, it is not considered alive till the start() method has been invoked on the thread instance. But since it is not dead or locked, it is available to run and hence in the Runnable state. The thread scheduler is responsible to move it to the Running state whenever it is requested from the Runnable pool to run a process.

73: When does a thread enter into the dead state?

Answer:

As soon as its run method completes, it gets to dead state.

74: You have a single-processor machine. How many threads can be made running at a time?

Answer:

There can only be one thread in running state. Although, many thread(s) may be in the Runnable state.

75: Does the order in which threads were started determine the order in which they'll run?

Answer:

No. There is no such guarantee.

76: Do threads take turns in any fair way?

Answer:

No. It is the thread scheduler which schedules the threads and it is determined by the particular virtual machine implementation.

77: How can you guarantee that your threads will take turns regardless of the underlying JVM?

Answer:

You need to use sleep() method in order to prevent thread starvation.

78: You invoked sleep() method on your thread to delay its exception for some time. Will it start running as soon as the sleep period is over?

Answer:

There is no such guarantee. The thread will sleep for at least the time specified in the argument to the sleep() method (interruption is an exception to that) but there is no guarantee that it will come to running state as soon as it gets awakened.

79: What is thread priority and how can you define it?

Answer:

Thread priority is way to tell the OS how much resource should be given to each thread. Thread priority can be set using Thread.setPriority(int). A thread's priority varies from 1 to 10 with 10 being the highest priority.

80: What is the default priority of a thread?

Answer:

A thread gets the same priority as of the thread that created it.

81: What is the purpose of join() method?

Answer:

ThreadA will call join() method of ThreadB if ThreadA wants to wait until ThreadB has completed, i.e. ThreadA can only start working after ThreadB has finished its work.

82: You have a method that has some critical code that you wish to protect from multiple threads' simultaneous execution. What can you do to protect it?

Answer:

Such method can be made synchronized by using the synchronized keyword as a method modifier.

83: Does a sleeping thread release all its locks?

Answer:

No. Sleeping thread's locks remain unavailable to other threads.

84: How you can synchronize a block of code i.e. not whole method?

Answer:

To synchronize a block of code, we have to specify an argument, that is, the object whose lock is to be synchronized on.

85: What does wait method do?

Answer:

wait() method puts the thread in the waiting pool. This thread remains there until notified using notify() method.

86: Can the notify() method specify which waiting thread to notify?

Answer:

No. wait() method sends a signal to only one of the threads waiting in the object's waiting pool.

87: What is the difference between notify() and notifyAll() methods?

Answer:

notifyAll() sends signal to all of the threads waiting on the object where as notify() sends signal to only one of threads waiting in the object's waiting pool.

88: Is it must to call wait(), notify() and notifyAll() from within synchronized context?

Answer:

Yes. A thread must hold the lock on that particular object when calling wait(), notify() or notifyAll().

89: What is the difference between wait and sleep methods?

Answer:

The static sleep () method moves the thread into the 'Not Runnable' state for a specific amount of time as specified in the method. It is called on the thread. The wait () method is called on an object and not the thread. It moves the thread containing the object into the 'Not Runnable' state indefinitely till the notify () method is invoked on it. The wait () method is synchronized while the sleep () method is not.

90: Can you override Thread start()method?

Answer:

Yes. It is not final and can be overridden but this should not be done.

This page is intentionally left blank.

Chapter 5

Servlet

91: Explain the life cycle of a Servlet.

Answer:

The servlet's life cycle involves five stages:

a) The classloader loads the Servlet class when the web container requests it
b) The web container creates a single instance of a Servlet
c) The init() method is called by the web container to initialize the Servlet. This happens only once in the lifecycle of a Servlet.
d) The web container calls the service() method every time the Servlet is requested. It checks whether the Servlet is initialized or not. If the Servlet is not yet initialised, the first 3 steps are executed and then the service() method is invoked. The first 3 steps happen only once in the lifecycle of a Servlet.

e) The web container invokes the destroy() method before removing the instance of the Servlet from the server. It gives a chance to the Servlet for garbage collection and cleaning up any open threads etc.

92: How to create a Servlet? Explain with code.

Answer:

A Servlet can be created in three ways:

a) Implement the Servlet Interface
b) Inherit the GenericServlet class
c) Inherit the HttpServlet class

The most commonly used method is the to inherit the HttpServlet class since it provides the basic methods to handle form data with doGet(), doPut(), doHead(), doPost() etc.

Sample code:

```
import javax.servlet.http.*;  // import the http package
import javax.servlet.*;  // import the servlet package
import java.io.*;  // import the Input / Output package for the printer stream
public class myFirstServlet extends HttpServlet{
    public void doGet(HttpServletRequest myServletRequest,HttpServletResponse myServletResponse)
        throws ServletException,IOException {  // since it throws IOException
            myServletResponse.setContentType("text/html");//setting the content type
            PrintWriter prntWrtr =
            myServletResponse.getWriter();//get the stream to
```

```
            write the data
            prntWrtr.println("<html><body>");
            prntWrtr.println("Welcome to Java Servlets");
            prntWrtr.println("</body></html>");
            prntWrtr.close();//closing the stream
        }
    }
}
```

93: What are Servlet Filters? How do they help Servlet Programming?

Answer:

The Servlet Filters are basically Java classes used in Servlet programming. They help to interpret the client requests before giving access to the backend resource. They also get to manipulate or tweak the results before it is sent to the client. There are around 9 Servlet filters commonly in use. They are Authentication Filters, Data compression Filters, Image Conversion Filters, Filters that trigger resource access events, Encryption Filters, XSL/T Filters That Transform XML Content, MIME-TYPE Chain Filters, Tokenizing Filters, Logging and Auditing Filters and XSL/T Filters That Transform XML Content. A java class implementing the javax.servlet.Filter is specified as the filter in the web.xml file. Each time the web application is requested; the Servlet container will check the request and decide the appropriate filter to apply and add them in the same order as they are mentioned in the web.xml file. The filter is also like a Servlet and has its own life cycle just like the Servlet. The filter has its own init() doFilter() and destroy() methods.

94: Explain Session tracking in Servlets.

Answer:

Session means basically a period of time. Session tracking means tracking a particular user's request. Each time a user posts a request it is considered as a new session or a new request. This is made possible with Hidden or invisible form fields, Cookies, HttpSession and URL rewriting.

a) **Hidden Form Fields** – these are text fields which are not displayed to the user in the user interface. But they are invisible and are available in the form which is used to store data. When the form is submitted, even if cookies are disabled, the data stored in the hidden field can be used for session tracking. The main disadvantage is that it is stored in the server.

b) **Cookies** are information stored in the browser on the client side. So every time the client requests, the cookie data also comes along with the request which helps the server to identify the client easily. The main disadvantage is that cookies can be disabled in the browser citing security reasons.

c) **HttpSession** is the most commonly used method to handle user sessions. Using the HttpServletRequest's getSession() method the current session of the user can be retrieved or if a session id has not been created, it will create a new session id and return the same. HttpSession interface has some useful methods like getId() that returns the session Id as a string, getCreationTime() which returns the time in milliseconds when this session was created, getLastAccessedTime() which returns the last time when the client sent a request associated with this session in milliseconds, invalidate() that invalidates the current session and unbinds any bound objects.

d) **URL Rewriting** technique works by adding tokens and values along with the URL during the submission. The main advantage here is that form submission is not required. It will work with links and is browser independent. But only textual information can be passed and the user can view the information thus passed. Example: url?key1=value1&key2=value2

95: Differentiate between ServletContext and ServletConfig.

Answer:

ServletContext is shared by all Servlets belonging to an application on one JVM. It is specific to one application and all Servlets in this application can access the ServletContext. It contains the access details of all Servlets within the application and uses the information and methods in it to communicate with other Servlets within the application. ServletConfig deals with the configuration details of the Servlet. It is like a deployment descriptor which is specific to each Servlet. Even if the configuration information of the Servlet is changed from the web.xml file, we don't have to modify the Servlet. So it is much easier to manage the Servlet even if the content is changed periodically.

96: How to unload a Servlet?

Answer:

You can manually unload the Servlet or simply shutdown the server.

97: Assume that you have deployed a Servlet on a web container. When does it get loaded?

Answer:

If auto-load is not enabled; the Servlet gets loaded on the first request. When auto-load is enabled, Servlet is loaded on server startup.

98: Which web.xml tag is used to define the Servlet loading order?

Answer:

load-on-startup tag is used to define the Servlet loading order.

99: Can you instantiate a Servlet class by using new keyword?

Answer:

No. Servlet container is responsible for instantiating the Servlet and only it can call the constructor.

100: A GET request is made to your Servlet and doGet() method will be invoked. How will the parameter be received?

Answer:

Parameters are appended to the URL in Get request and are not encrypted. HttpServletRequest.getParameter("paramName") is used to get the parameter values.

101: A POST request is made to your Servlet and doPost() method will be invoked. How will the parameter be received?

Answer:

Parameters are sent through a socket back to the WebServer. These parameters are not shown in the URL and are encrypted. HttpServletRequest.getParameter("paramName") is used to get the parameter values.

102: In which scenario doGet() is to be used?

Answer:

doGet() is to be used when request is made to read data only. They are not supposed to add or update any data on the server.

103: In which scenario doPost() is to be used?

Answer:

doPost() is used to update or add information to the server.

104: When comparing doGet with doPost, which one is faster?

Answer:

doGet is faster than doPost.

105: What is the data limitation of GET request?

Answer:

URL can contain maximum of 1024 characters.

106: Name the phases of Servlet life cycle.

Answer:

The phases of Servlet life cycle are:

a) Servlet class loading
b) Servlet instantiation
c) Servlet initialization
d) Request handling
e) Removal of service

107: Can you call doPost manually from a doGet method?

Answer:

Yes. We can delegate a request from doGet to doPost. e.g.

```
public void doGet(HttpServletRequest request,
HttpServletResponse response) throws ServletException,
IOException
{
    doPost(request, response);
}
```

108: Why should I not override the service() method in my HttpServlet?

Answer:

Usually it is not good to override it since HttpServlet does it and the default service method invokes the doXXX depending on the request made.

109: Which one is faster? forward() or sendRedirect() ?

Answer:

forward is a bit faster than redirect. The reason is, redirect requires two browser requests instead of one for forward.

110: sendRedirect() is a two phase process, which are those

phases?

Answer:

Phase 1 - Browser makes a request to the server. Server instructs the browser to fetch a different URL

Phase 2 - Browser makes another request.

111: Why is original request context retained in forward()?

Answer:

The original request is retained because both the resources are part of same context.

112: You want to redirect a request to another resource that is in the some other domain. Will you use forward()?

Answer:

No. sendDirect() is to used since the actual resource does not belong to the current context.

113: Where does Servlet run?

Answer:

Servlet runs inside a web container. Example: Tomcat.

114: Which protocols are supported by Java Servlet?

Answer:

Java Servlet can support any protocol.

Example: HTTP, FTP, SMTP etc.

115: How session tracking is done by Servlet container?

Answer:

Session tracking is done using Cookies, URL rewriting, HttpSession, Hidden form fields, etc.

116: Define session mapping.

Answer:

An association between a URL pattern and a Servlet is maintained using Session Mapping. This mapping is used to map requests to Servlets.

117: Define Servlet context.

Answer:

Information about the Web application and container is contained in an object called Servlet context.

118: I want to initialize Servlet using constructor instead of init(). Will I have access to ServletConfig to ServletContext?

Answer:

Servlet specific things like ServletConfig or ServletContext are not available in the constructor. You can write a constructor that takes ServletConfig as a parameter but Servlet container will always call no-argument constructor.

119: How do you get the current Servlet path i.e. its location on file system?

Answer:

Servlet's file system location can be found using the following:

request.getRealPath(request.getServletPath());

120: When does init() method gets called?

Answer:

init() method is called when the Servlet is loaded. It is called once per Servlet instance.

121: How to make init() method thread safe?

Answer:

Since init() is called once per Servlet instance, we do not need to worry about thread safety.

122: How can you call a Servlet from another Servlet?

Answer:

There are various ways of doing so. For instance: you can use a RequestDispatcher, send a redirect, etc.

123: Give an example to show how RequestDispatcher can be used to forward a request from one Servlet to another.

Answer:

```
..
RequestDispatcher rd =
request.getRequestDispatcher("http://test.com/ServletB");
String myAttribute = "Test Attribute";
request.setAttribute("att1", myAttribute);
rd.forward(request, response);
..
```

124: What is the difference between request.getParameter() and request.getAttribute() where request is an instance of

javax.Servlet.http.HttpServletRequest?

Answer:

request.getParameter() is used to get the value posted by a form. request.getAttribute() is used only on the server side. You can add an attribute to the request and forward that request to another resource.

125: How can you access client's directory structure from a Servlet?

Answer:

This is not possible due to security reasons.

126: What are Generic Servlets?

Answer:

Generic Servlets are protocol independent Servlets.

127: What is the difference between Generic and HttpServlet Servlet?

Answer:

HttpServlet is type of Generic Servlet. It provides Http specific functionality where as Generic Servlet is protocol independent.

128: Is HttpServlet a concrete class?

Answer:

No. It is an Abstract class that extends GenericServlet.

129: Since HttpServlet is an Abstract class, which methods it must override?

Answer:

HttpServlet must override at least one of the following methods: doGet(), doPost(), doPut(), doDelete(), init(), destroy(), getServletInfo()

130: Who controls the life cycle of a Servlet?

Answer:

Servlet container is responsible for controlling the life cycle of a Servlet.

131: When a request is mapped to a Servlet, what does the container do?

Answer:

Assuming that the Servlet instance does not exist, the container loads the Servlet class, creates its instance, initializes the servlet by calling the init() method. Once that is done, service method is called and request and response objects are passed to it.

132: Which method is invoked by the container once it needs to remove the Servlet?

Answer:

Destroy method is called in order to remove the Servlet.

133: What is the purpose of service method?

Answer:

GenericServlet class has an abstract service method that takes ServletRequest and ServletResponse as parameters. HttpServlet overrides it and dispatches the client request to the protected service method that takes HttpServletRequest and HttpServletResponse as parameters. This method dispatches the request to doXXX.

134: You want to write a Servlet for Http protocol. Which class you need to extend?

Answer:

HttpServlet will be extended to create an HttpServlet.

Example:

```
public class HelloServlet extends HttpServlet {
```

135: Which exceptions are thrown by the doXXX methods?

Answer:

javax.Servlet.ServletException and java.io.IOException.

136: Where you can define Servlet mapping?

Answer:

Servlet mapping is defined in WEB-INF/web.xml.

137: How can you define context init parameter in web.xml?

Answer:

You can create Context init parameters in web.xml using the context-param tags.

Example:

```
<context-param>
    <param-name>EmployeeName</param-name>
    <param-value>Johhny Bravo</param-value>
</context-param>
```

```
<context-param>
    <param-name>EmployeePwd</param-name>
    <param-value>P@$$word</param-value>
</context-param>
```

This creates two init parameters EmployeeName and EmployeePwd with values given against the <param-value> tag for each respectively.

138: How can you retrieve context init parameters in Servlet?

Answer:

To retrieve context init parameters, we need ServletConfig reference:

```
ServletContext context = getServletContext();
dbName = context.getInitParameter("name");
dbPassword = context.getInitParameter("password");
```

139: How can you set error page in web.xml?

Answer:

```
<error-page>
<error-code>404</error-code>
<location>/404.html</location>
</error-page>
```

140: Give an example of Servlet mapping in web.xml.

Answer:

Assuming that Servlet class name is MyServletTrial and we can to access it using /Test:

```
<web-app>
```

```
    <Servlet>
        <Servlet-name>MyServletTrialName</Servlet-name>
        <Servlet-class>MyServletTrial</Servlet-class>
    </Servlet>
    <Servlet-mapping>
        <Servlet-name>MyServletTrialName</Servlet-name>
        <url-pattern>/ServletTest</url-pattern>
    </Servlet-mapping>
</web-app>
```

141: Define ServletContext.

Answer:

It is an interface that is used to communicate with Servlet container. There exists only one ServletContext per web application. All resource in the web application shares that ServletContext.

142: Will all the Servlets in a web application share the same ServletConfig?

Answer:

No. Each Servlet will have its own ServletConfig.

143: What methods are provided by ServletContextListener interface?

Answer:

ServletContextListener interface provides two methods:

public void contextInitialized(ServletContextEvent event)

public void contextDestroyed(ServletContextEvent event)

If we implement ServletContextListener, we have to implement both of these.

144: When does ServletContextListener gets notified?

Answer:

ServletContextListener gets notified when ServletContext is initialized and it gets init parameters from the ServletContext. ServletContextListener also gets notified when the ServletContext gets destroyed.

145: How to configure ServletContextListener in web.xml?

Answer:

Assume that ServletContextListenerExample implements ServletContextListener:

```
<web-app>
<listener>
<listener-class>example.ServletContextListenerExample
</listener-class>
</listener>
</web-app>
```

146: When deploying Servlet on a web container, what is the purpose of WEB-INF?

Answer:

WEB-INF should contain web.xml and a classes folder with Servlet class files.

147: What will happen if I want to use the Servlet 2.1 API

instead of Servlet2.0 API?

Answer:

If we use Servlet 2.1 API instead of Servlet 2.0 API, servlet to servlet communication will not work since communication using servletcontext methods like getServlet() and getServlets() have been deprecated. It will return null.

148: What is lazy loading in servlet?

Answer:

The servlet container will not load/initialize the servlet by default when the server gets started. It will load/initialize the servlet when it receives a request for that servlet for the first time. This is lazy loading.

149: How will you call a servlet along with the parameters in the URL?

Answer:

We can call a servlet along with the parameters using the form, http://localhost:8080/servlet?param1=servlet1||param2=servlet2

Chapter 6

Collections

150: Differentiate between Hashtable and Hashmap.

Answer:

Though they sound similar, the Hashtable and Hashmap have a lot of differences:

In terms of the Null Values, Hashmap allows one null key and many null values but the Hashtable object does not allow any null key or null value. Another major difference is characterized by the way Synchronization or Thread-Safety is handled in Hashmap and Hashtable. A Hashmap is not synchronized and hence not thread-safe. So it is not recommended in multi-threading applications. A Hashtable is synchronized and thread-safe and hence it can be used in applications where multi-threading is required. Hashmap uses the iterator to access the object values. Hashtable uses an Enumerator to iterate the values in the object. Since the Hashmaps are not synchronized, they perform much better than the Hashtables which are synchronized. The iterators are considered more fail-fast than the enumerators. So the possibility of Hashmap's iterator throwing an exception or error is more than the Hashtable's enumerator. Hashtable is a subclass of Dictionary class which is no longer used in Java. Hashmap is the subclass of AbstractMap class in Java which is still in use. These are the major differences between Hashmaps and Hashtables.

151: Explain how Hashmap works in Java.

Answer:

Hashmap works on the principle of hashing. Hashing involves Bucket, Hash function and Hash value. Bucket stores the pairs of key and value. It is like a simple linked-list that stores multiple key-value pair of objects. Hash function or the hashCode() method returns the Hash value of the Hashmap. It is an integer value. The get(Key keyVal) function in a Hashmap is used to return the value stored against the keyVal. Since Hashmaps allow one null Key, the get() method first checks whether the keyVal is null or not and then returns the value associated with the key. If Key is null, then it maps to the index 0. The set of Keys and Values are stored in a bucket location which is essentially an array where the keys and values are stored as Entry objects. The Entry object in a bucket stores the hash, key, value and the bucketindex. If more than one key has the same hash code, the equals() method determines the right value to return.

152: Differentiate between Comparable and Comparator.

Answer:

Both Comparable and Comparator are used to sort collection elements. But the following differences are there:

a) Comparable allows sorting based on only a single element like name whereas Comparator allows sorting based on multiple elements like name, class, age etc.
b) Comparable modifies the actual class whereas Comparator does not modify the actual class.
c) Comparable uses compareTo() method to compare and sort the elements whereas Comparator uses compare() method to sort the elements.
d) Comparable is a part of java.lang package while the Comparator is a part of the java.uitl package.
e) Comparable type list elements can be sorted with Collections.sort(List) method. Comparator type list elements are sorted with Collections.sort(List,Comparator) method.

153: Explain the output of the program.

```
import java.util.Hashmap;
import java.util.Map;

public class myMapTrial{
        public static void main(String abcs[]){
            Map myMap1 = new HashMap();
            myMap1.put(null, "testvalue");
            myMap1.put(null,"Festvalue");
            System1.out.println(myMap);
        }
```

}

Answer:

The result will be {null == Festvalue} as the Java Hashmap allows only one null key which is the last added key value pair. If you add more keys and values, it will also be displayed along with the null key-value pair. For example, if you add before printing,

myMap.put(1," value1");
myMap.put(2," value2");

the result will be {null == Festvalue, 1 == value1, 2 == value2}

154: Differentiate – Iterator, ListIterator and Enumerator.

Answer:

Enumeration interface is a legacy interface. It can navigate in forward course only. It uses the elements() method which returns an Enumerator. You can traverse through and retrieve the enumerators elements using the hasMoreElement() and nextElement() methods. It takes in null value also.

Iterator is implemented in all java collections and uses the iterator() method. Iterator also can navigate in forward direction only. You can access the elements in an Iterator with hasNext(), next() and remove() methods.

ListIterator is required only for List classes. It uses the listIterator() method. ListIterator an traverse in both directions. The ListIterator uses hasNext(), next(), previous(), hasPrevious(), remove(), nextIndex(), and previousIndex() methods to access the elements.

155: Both ArrayList and LinkedList implements get(int) method to fetch an object at specified position in list. Which one is faster?

Answer:

ArrayList's get(int) is faster as compared to LinkedList's get(int) since in case of LinkedList it just iterates over the list until it reaches the index specified.

156: Why adding elements to ArrayList can be slow?

Answer:

Adding elements in ArrayList is slow when size of elements in unknown. When the size of ArrayList expands because of adding elements, a lot of shifting is done in the memory.

157: You want to add an element in the middle of a List. Which List implementation gives you better performance? LinkedList or ArrayList?

Answer:

In case of manipulation, LinkedList is faster. In LinkedList, we may add an element at a specified position and internally a node will be created and two links will be changed. In case of ArrayList, a lot of shifting is done in the memory when an element is added in the middle of the List or anywhere except at the end.

158: You want a List whose size will grow with time. You may also need to add elements in between existing elements but you will very seldom need random access. Which List implementation you will prefer?

Answer:

LinkedList is the right choice in the given scenario.

159: Hashtable defines the following constructor: Hashtable(int initialCapacity, float loadFactor) What is initialCapacity and loadFactor here?

Answer:

These are to enhance performance. initialCapacity defines the capacity of Hashtable at the time of creation. The capacity of Hashtable is automatically increased when the Hashtable gets full. How much full the Hashtable is allowed to get is the loadFactor.

160: What is the Hashtable default load factor?

Answer:

The default load factor for Hashtable is .75.

161: What will be the initial capacity of Hashtable if it is created using: public Hashtable()

Answer:

By default, the initial capacity of Hashtable is 11.

162: What is the difference between Hashtable and HashMap?

Answer:

The main differences between Hashtable and HashMap are:

a) Hashtable is synchronized where as Hashmap is unsynchronized
b) Hashtable is does not permit null where as Hashmap permits null

163: You use the following to get an Object from a HashMap.
public Object get(Object key)
What happens of the specified key is not present in the HashMap?

Answer:

If the map contains no mapping for the key, null is returned. The following method is useful to make sure that the key exists in the map:

public boolean containsKey(Object key)

164: You have a HashMap and want to get a collection view of the mappings contained in this map? Which method will you invoke?

Answer:

entrySet() is to be invoked that return a Set. Each element in the returned set will be a Map.Entry.

All the changes made in the collection will be reflected in the HashMap and vice-versa.

165: Is Map a Collection?

Answer:

The Map interface is a pair of Keys and corresponding Values. It does not extend the Collection interface and hence, it is not a collection. You can always create a collection of maps as in a list of maps to store a collection of related key-value pairs.

166: What happens if you try to add a duplicate key in a Map?

Answer:

The corresponding value will be over written and the old value will be lost.

167: Which Map implementation will you use if you need to insert, delete, and locate elements in a Map?

Answer:

HashMap offers the best alternative for inserting, deleting, and locating elements in a Map.

168: In which case will you prefer TreeMap over HashMap?

Answer:

If traversing keys in a sorted order is required, then TreeMap is a better alternative.

169: How can you tune HashMap and TreeMap?

Answer:

For HashMap, you need to create your HashMap with proper initial capacity and load factor for better performance. The TreeMap has no tuning options.

170: You want to create a single element set using Collection class. How you will do it in a single line of code?

Answer:

Set set = Collection.singleton("Test Msg");

171: What happens if hash value of the key in the map collides with an existing key in the Map?

Answer:

In that case, the Map will re-arrange and will keep the keys in a list under that hash. hashCode() and equals() method of the Class to which the key belongs to, plays an important role here.

172: What are the two ways to traverse a collection?

Answer:

You may traverse a collection either by using for-each construct or by using Iterators.

173: Assume that you are traversing a Collection using an Iterator. Can you remove items from the Collection using its Iterator? If yes, how to?

Answer:

Iterator provides remove method that removes the last element that was returned by next method. For example, the following removes 'Test2' from the List using Iterator.

```
List<String> myStringList = new ArrayList<String>();
myStringList.add("Test1");
myStringList.add("Test2");
myStringList.add("Test3");

Iterator<String> myListIterator = myStringList.iterator();
while(myListIterator.hasNext()){
    String val = myListIterator.next();
    if(val.equals("Test2")){
        myListIterator.remove();
    }
}
```

174: With respect to collections, what does build operation mean?

Answer:

Performing some operation on the entire collection is referred as Build Operation. For example, you can clear a collection using the clear().

```
List<String> myStringList = new ArrayList<String>();
myStringList.add("Test1");
myStringList.add("Test2");
myStringList.add("Test3");
myStringList.clear();
```

175: Which bulk operations are supported by Collection interface?

Answer:

Collection interface supports following bulk operations:
containsAll, addAll, removeAll, retainAll, clear

176: I have a Collection called 'c' and want to remove all the null elements from it. How should I do it using build operation?

Answer:

```
c.removeAll(Collections.singleton(null));
```

Collections.singleton is used to get an immutable Set containing only the specified element.

177: How can we convert a Collection to an Array?

Answer:

Collection interface provides toArray() method to translate a

Collection on an Array.

Example:

Object[] a = c.toArray();

178: You have a Collection of String type and want to convey it into an Array of String type. How can this be achieved?

Answer:

c.toArray() will always return an array of type Object. To get an Array of type String, the following is to be used:

String[] myArray = myStringList.toArray(new String[0]);

The size of myArray will be equal to the size of myStringList.

179: Name the three general-purpose Set implementations.

Answer:

a) HashSet,
b) TreeSet, and
c) LinkedHashSet.

180: Which java.util.Set implementation is the fastest one?

Answer:

HashSet is faster as compared to TreeSet and LinkedHashSet.

181: Which java.util.Set implementation does not guarantee the order of the elements?

Answer:

HashSet

182: How java.util.TreeSet stores its elements?

Answer:

In TreeSet, elements are stored as red-black tree and are ordered based on their values.

183: You have a Collection called 'c' that contains duplicates. How can you remove those using Set?

Answer:

Assume that 'c' is a collection of type String and contains duplicates.

```
Collection<String> noDuplicates = new HashSet<String>(c);
```

184: You have a Collection called 'c' that contains duplicates. How can you remove those using Set but want to the order of elements?

Answer:

Assume that 'c' is a collection of type String and contains duplicates.

```
Collection<String> noDuplicates = new LinkedHashSet<String>(c);
```

185: How can you get cardinality of a Set?

Answer:

size() method returns the number of elements present in a Set.

186: What happens if you try to add an element that already exists in the Set?

Answer:

Since duplicates are not allowed in Set, adding an item that already exists in a Set will fail.

187: What happens if you try to remove an item from a Set that does not exist in the Set?

Answer:

There will be no exception thrown. The remove method will return FALSE.

188: Name the java.util.Set implementation that orders the elements based on their insertion order.

Answer:

LinkedHashSet

189: You have two sets namely set1 and set2. You want to do union operation in order to add set2 into set1. Which bulk operation you will use?

Answer:

addAll operation will serve the purpose.

Example: set1.addAll(set2);

190: You have two sets namely set1 and set2: You want to remove all elements of set2 from set1. Which bulk operation you will use?

Answer:

removeAll operation will serve the purpose.

set1.removeAll(set2);

191: Can a List contain duplicates?

Answer:

Yes, it can contain duplicates.

192: Apart from inherited operations from Collection interface, what additional operations are provided by List?

Answer:

List interface provides: Positional access, Search, Iteration, Range-view.

193: Name few of the algorithms supported my List.

Answer:

Sort, shuffle, reverse, rotate, swap, replaceAll, fill, copy, binarySearch, indexOfSubList, lastIndexOfSubList

194: There are two forms of Queue methods depending on the operation failure. Name them.

Answer:

There are queue methods that throw exception if operation fails.
Example: add(e), remove(), element().
There are queue methods that return a special value if operation fails.
Example: offer(e), poll(), peek().

195: What are bounded queues?

Answer:

If a queue restricts the number of elements in it, it is referred as a Bounded Queue.

196: Which Java package contains bounded queues and which one contains un-bounded queues?

Answer:

Java's util package contains Queue implementations that are not bounded. But the Queue implementations in java's concurrent class are bounded.

197: You have an empty Queue and you try to remove an element using poll(). What will be the result?

Answer:

poll() will return null in case the Queue is empty.

198: What will be the outcome of remove() operation conducted on an empty Queue?

Answer:

NoSuchElementException will be thrown.

199: You want to get the head element of a Queue. What methods can you use?

Answer:

element() and peek() methods can be used to get the head elements on a Queue.

200: What is the difference between element() and peek() methods of Queue?

Answer:

peek() returns the head element of the Queue without removing it whereas element() returns and removes the head element of the Queue.

201: Name the Queue implementations that allow insertion of null elements.

Answer:

The LinkedList implementation allows insertion of null elements.

202: Do Queue implementations generally define element-based versions of the equals and hashCode methods?

Answer:

No. Queue implementations generally inherit the identity-based versions of equals and hashCode methods from Object.

203: In concurrent programming, blocking queue methods are required. Does Queue interface provide that?

Answer:

No. Queue interface does not provide blocking queue methods. However java.util.concurrent.BlockingQueue, which extends Queue, provides that.

204: Name the general-purpose Map implementations.

Answer:

HashMap, TreeMap, and LinkedHashMap.

205: When comparing Map with Hashtable, which one of these provides the functionality to remove entries in the midst of iteration?

Answer:

Hashtable

206: How do you differentiate between Vector and ArrayList?

Answer:

Vector is synchronized version of ArrayList. If synchronization is not your concern, then using ArrayList is a better option.

207: What is the difference between Collection and Collections?

Answer:

Collection is an interface from which Set and List extend. Collections is a class that holds static utility methods for Collection.

208 Define the java.util.Vector class.

Answer:

Vector is a Serializable class that represents a growable array of objects.

209: What is an Iterator interface?

Answer:

If you want to iterate through a collection, then iterator interface it to be used.

210: Event handling is supported by which java.util classes and interfaces?

Answer:

java.util.EventObject class and the java.utilEventListener interface support event processing.

211: What is the java.util.Map?

Answer:

Map represents key value pair where key in a map has to be unique. Following classes implement Map: AbstractMap,

Attributes, HashMap, Hashtable, IdentityHashMap, RenderingHints, TreeMap, WeakHashMap

212: What is the highest-level event class of the event-delegation model?

Answer:

The highest-level class in the event-delegation class hierarchy is the Java.util.EventObject class.

213: What is the difference between the size and capacity of a Vector?

Answer:

The maximum number of elements that a vector can store at a given instance is called capacity of that vector class where as the total number of elements in a vector class is referred as size of that vector class.

Chapter 7

Design Patterns

214: What are Design Patterns and what types of Design Patterns do Java has?

Answer:

Design patterns are like best coding principles meant to help the software developers during the development stage. These patterns or solutions were formed from the trial and error of various software developers over a considerable period of time. Following the design patterns, the software developers can solve many common issues faced during the development stage. Design patterns are basically categorized into three –

a) **Creational Patterns** – helps to create objects efficiently while hiding the logic. It is against instantiating an object during creation. The program can decide when to create an object based on the requirements.

b) **Structural Patterns** – helps with defining classes and objects. More importance is given to inheritance and implementation of interfaces. During implementation they can define how the object behaves for new functionalities.

c) **Behavioural Patterns** – helps in how objects communicate with each other.

d) **J2EE Patterns** - helps with the presentation layer of the Java architecture

215: Explain the MCV Pattern.

Answer:

The MCV or Model-View Controller pattern helps in separating the various application components such as the data, its presentation and the controller. Model is an object or the data. It can also be a process that updates the controller when data changes. View is how the data is represented in front of the user. It can be considered as the user interface also.

Controller is responsible for the data flow into the model object and updates the View every time the data changes. It mediates between the model and the view and keeps them separate. In a web application's context, model is the server which has the data, view is the user interface or GUI and the controller is the DataManager. When the user requests some data over the GUI, the DataManager takes the request and searches the server for the requested information and returns it to the user.

216: Explain Factory Method in Creational pattern.

Answer:

The Factory Method is one of the most popular design patterns as it provides a framework of the functionalities involved in a particular application which can be implemented differently for each purpose. This is most useful when the program requires following a hierarchy. For example – Shape is a class that can be a superclass for circle, square, rectangle etc. So create an interface for Shape with a method to draw() the shape. Create classes for Circle, Square and Rectangle which implements the interface Shape. The draw() method has to be overridden in each class in a different way to return a Shape. When a program requires this type of hierarchy and functionality, the Factory Method design pattern can be followed.

217: Explain the Proxy design pattern.

Answer:

Proxy pattern is useful when creating the actual object or a process is very time or memory consuming. Using the proxy you can postpone the actual creation until it is absolutely necessary. Proxy pattern is commonly used while loading a large image, loading huge volume of data over a network during peak traffic or while the user waits for a complex authentication process to complete. The 'loading' image or the hourglass is a classic example of Proxy. It is related to the Adapter pattern and Decorator pattern. While the Adapter pattern supplies a new interface to the adapted object, the Proxy pattern uses the same interface. The Decorator pattern adds new functions or decorates the object with new functions while a Proxy controls the right to use the existing object.

218: Explain Data Access Object or DAO.

Answer:

The DAO or Data Access Object provides a standard API for accessing different types of relational, object-oriented and un-relational databases. This makes data access easier to the developer. It basically involves 3 components –

a) Data Access Object Interface which describes the general operations to be executed on a model object.
b) Data Access Object concrete class that implements above the DAO interface. This class actually retrieves the data from the database or xml file or any other data storage.
c) Value Object or Model Object which is a simple Plain Old Java Object that contains the get() and set() methods to retrieve and store the data using the DAO class.

219: Explain the Intercepting Filter pattern.

Answer:

An Intercepting filter pattern is used when there is a need for pre-processing of data before a request is submitted or post-processing of data after the response is returned to the application. The basic authorisation or tracking can be done using filters. These filters are applied to the request before passing on to the application which actually processes the request. The Intercepting filter pattern consists of the following entities:

a) The Filter that performs the filter conditions before or after executing the request handler's request.
b) The Filter chain which has multiple filters defined and executed in an order.
c) The Target which is the request handler

d) The Filter Manager which manages the filters and the filter chain
e) The Client which is essentially an object that sends the request to the Target object

220: In which cases using Proxy pattern is preferred?

Answer:

When creating an object is expensive in terms of time and memory, proxy object is created and used.

221: What is Facade pattern?

Answer:

Facade pattern is used to provide a general interface to make complex system simpler. This actually hides the complexities of the system by decoupling the subsystems.

222: What is the other name for Adapter pattern?

Answer:

Adapter pattern is also referred as Wrapper pattern.

223: You wish to convert the existing interfaces to a new interface in order to achieve compatibility and reusability of the unrelated classes in your legacy application. Which design pattern will you use?

Answer:

Adapter pattern can be used since it is used to make unrelated classes work together.

224: You want to add operations on a bunch of classes which have different interfaces. Which design pattern is to be applied?

Answer:

Visitor pattern is to be applied.

225: Which design pattern is used to return one of several factories?

Answer:

Abstract Factory Pattern provides one level of interface higher than the factory pattern.

226: What is Singleton pattern? Give code example.

Answer:

Singleton pattern is used when you wish to have exactly one instance of a class.

Example:

```
public class ClassA {
    private static ClassA instance = null;
    private ClassA() {
    }
    public static ClassA getInstance() {
        if(instance == null) {
            instance = new ClassA();
        }
        return instance;
    }
}
```

Chapter 8

Data Structures

227: How do you find the middle element in a linked list in one pass?

Answer:

Generally we have to traverse through a list once to find the length of the list and then find the middle element in the second time. But since we have to do it in one pass, we have to use 2 pointers. The 1st pointer will increment on each iteration and the 2nd pointer will increment on every 2nd iteration. Thus when the 1st pointer will point to the end of the list, the 2nd pointer will point to the middle of the list. Code implementing the logic is given below:

```
public class myLinkedListTrial {
    public static void main(String abcs[]) {
        //creating LinkedList with 7 elements including head
        LinkedList myLinkedList = new LinkedList();
```

```
LinkedList.Node headNode = myLinkedList.head();

myLinkedList.add( new LinkedList.Node("a"));
myLinkedList.add( new LinkedList.Node("b"));
myLinkedList.add( new LinkedList.Node("c"));
myLinkedList.add( new LinkedList.Node("d"));
myLinkedList.add( new LinkedList.Node("e"));
myLinkedList.add( new LinkedList.Node("f"));

//find the middle element of LinkedList in single pass
LinkedList.Node currentNode = headNode;
int lengthArr = 0;
LinkedList.Node middleNode = headNode;

while(currentNode.next() != null){
    lengthArr++;
    if(lengthArr % 2 == 0){
        middleNode = middleNode.next();
    }
    currentNode = currentNode.next();
}

if(lengthArr % 2 == 1){
    middleNode = middleNode.next();
}

System.out.println("Actual Length of Linked List is : " +
lengthArr);
```

```
        System.out.println("Middle element of the Linked List is :
        " + middleNode);

    }
}
class LinkedList{
    private Node headNode;
    private Node tailNode;
    public LinkedList(){
        this.headNode = new Node("headNode");
        tailNode = headNode;
    }
    public Node head(){
        return headNode;
    }
    public void add(Node node1){
        tailNode.nextNode = node1;
        tailNode = node1;
    }
    public static class Node{
        private Node nextNode;
        private String dataStr;
        public Node(String dataStr){
            this.dataStr = dataStr;
        }
        public String data() {
            return dataStr;
        }
        public void setData(String dataStr) {
            this.dataStr = dataStr;
```

```
        }
        public Node next() {
            return nextNode;
        }
        public void setNext(Node nextNode) {
            this.nextNode = nextNode;
        }
        public String toString(){
            return this.dataStr;
        }
    }
}
```

Output:

Actual Length of Linked List is : 6

Middle element of the Linked List is : c

228: Explain the BubbleSort Algorithm with code.

Answer:

```
public class myBubbleSort {
    public static void main(String abcs[]) {
        //testing our bubble sort method in Java
        int[] unsortedArr = {23, 28,11, 34, 13, 3};
        myBubbleSort(unsorted);
        //Another array which is already sorted
        int[] testArr = { 10, 9, 8, 7};
        myBubbleSort (testArr);
    }
    public static void myBubbleSort(int[] unsortedArr){
```

```
        System.out.println("Array before sorting : " +
        Arrays.toString(unsortedArr));

        for(int itr=0; itr< unsortedArr.length -1; itr++){
            for(int jtr = 1; jtr < unsortedArr.length -itr; jtr++){
                //If current number is greater than swap those two
                if(unsortedArr [jtr-1] > unsortedArr [jtr]){
                    int tempVal = unsortedArr [jtr];
                    unsortedArr [jtr] = unsortedArr [jtr-1];
                    unsortedArr [jtr-1] = tempVal;
                }
            }
            System.out.printf("Array after %d pass %s: %n", itr+1,
            Arrays.toString(unsortedArr));
        }
    }
}
```

Output:

```
Array before sorting : [23, 28, 11, 34, 13, 3]
Array after 1 pass [23, 11, 28, 13, 3, 34]:
Array after 2 pass [11, 23, 13, 3, 28, 34]:
Array after 3 pass [11, 13, 3, 23, 28, 34]:
Array after 4 pass [11, 3, 13, 23, 28, 34]:
Array after 5 pass [3, 11, 13, 23, 28, 34]:
Array before sorting : [10, 9, 8, 7]
Array after 1 pass [9, 8, 7, 10]:
Array after 2 pass [8, 7, 9, 10]:
Array after 3 pass [7, 8, 9, 10]
```

229: Differentiate between Singly Linked List and Doubly Linked List.

Answer:

A singly linked list has only one pointer which points to the next element in the list. So only forward traversing is possible in Singly Linked List. In a Doubly Linked List, each element will have 2 pointers, one pointing to the next element and another pointing towards the previous element or null in case of the first element.

Singly Linked List

A ☞B☞C☞D

Here A has a pointer to B which has a pointer to C and C has a pointer to D.

Doubly Linked List

A☞☜B☞☜C☞☜D

Here A has only 1 pointer as it is the first element. B has 2 pointers 1 points to A and the other points to C. C also has 2 pointers, 1 pointing to B and the other to D. D also has only 1 pointer as it is the last element.

230: Explain a Binary Search Tree.

Answer:

A Binary Search Tree has some unusual characteristics. Left node of the binary tree is attached to the base or the root and the right node is attached to its sub nodes. The value of a right node is always greater than the root's value and the value on the left always has less than the root value. A Binary tree does not allow duplicate values. It is usually an ordered tree. Each node represents a record rather than a single element.

231: What are the classes included in the data structure of Java?

Answer:

The classes included in the data structure of Java are:

a) **Vector:** Class, similar to array
b) **Stack:** Class, Last In First Out method
c) **Enumeration:** An interface, retrieves the successive elements
d) **Bitset:** Class, creates group of bits/flag that can be set or cleared
e) **Dictionary:** Class, mapping of keys to the elements
f) **Hashtable:** Class, organization of data
g) **Properties:** Subclass of hash table, maintains the list that has both the value and key in String type

232: How will you 'AND' the contents of the two bitset?

Answer:

The contents of the two bitsets can be 'AND' by:

a) Using void and (BitSet my_bset1) function in bitset
b) Find the 'and' of invoking bitset with the specified bitset
c) Then the results are stored in the invoking bitset

233: How will you delete the elements from invokingbitset using specified bitset?

Answer:

The elements can be deleted from invokingbitset using specified bitset by:

a) Using void andNot(BitSet my_bset2) function in bitset
b) Element in the invoking bitset are deleted for the each

correspondoing one bit in the specified elements

234: How will you clear the bits in the BitSet?

Answer:

a) To clear all the bits, "void clear" method is used
b) To clear the bits from specified starting to end point, void clear "intmy_s_index, my_e_index" method is used
c) To clear the bit at specified position, "void clear(intmy_index_pos)" method is used

235: What is the purpose of the functions "clone" and "equals"?

Answer:

a) **Clone:** the invoked bitset objects will be duplicated
b) **Equals:** Returns true, when the bits in the invoked bitset matches with the one passed. Else false

236: Describe the "flip" function in the bitset.

Answer:

a) To complement the bits in the given range, "flip(int my_s_indes, int my_e_index)" method is used
b) To Complement the bit that is in the specified index, flip(int my_index1) is used

   Example:

      BitSet my_bset =new BitSet[];

      ...

      my_bset.flip(3,6) - bits from the index 3 to 6 are complemented

      my_bset.flip(7) - complements the bit in the 7th position

237: How will you get the current state and hash code for the bit?

Answer:

The current state and hash code for the bit can be got by:

a) Using 'get' function of return type 'Boolean', the state (True/false) of the bit which is at the specified index will be returned

b) Using 'hashCode' function of return type 'int', invoking object's hash code is returned

Example:

```
BitSet my_bset =new BitSet[];
...
my_bset .get(3);
my_bset .hashCode();
```

238: How will you get the string equivalent and size for the invoking bitset object?

Answer:

The string equivalent and size for the invoking bitset object can be got by:

a) Using'size' method of return type 'int', size of the invoked bitset is returned

b) Using 'toString' method of return type 'String', string equivalent of invoked object is returned

Example:

```
BitSet my_bset =new BitSet[];
...
my_bset.size();
```

```
my_bset.toString()
```

239: How will you add an element to the vector?

Answer:

An element can be added to the vector by:

a) Using 'add' function, given element is added at the specified position
b) Using 'addElement' method, given element is added at the end of the vector and size gets incremented

Example:

```
Vector my_vectr = new Vector[];
...
my_vectr.add(4 , 5); //Add the nuber '5' at the 4th postion
my_vectr.addElement(7);
```

240: How will you copy the component of a vector to an array?

Answer:

Using 'copyInto' function, the component of a vector can be copied to an array.

Example:

```
Vector my_vectr = new Vector(3);
int my_arrv2[] = new int[3];
...
my_vectr .copyInto(my_arrv2);
```

Copies the current component of the vector to the given 'my_arrv2' array.

241: What is the purpose of ensureCapacity function in vector?

Answer:

EnsureCapacity function in a vector checks the vector size and sets the size to the specified minimum value if it does not have the specified minimum length.

Example:

```
Vector my_vectr = new Vector[];
...
my_vectr .ensureCapacity(9);
```

242: Describe about remove and removeAll function.

Answer:

a) boolean remove(Object my_obj1) {}

   Deletes the first occurrence of the specified object in the vector.

b) booleanremoveAll(Collection my_col_obj) {}

   Deletes the elements that are in the specified collection.

243: Give an example for 'toArray' function.

Answer:

Example:

```
String my_elmt2[] = {"I", "C", "E"};
    Set my_set1 = new HashSet(Arrays.AsList(my_elmt2));
    String my_svar[] = new String(my_set1.size());
    my_svar = (toString) my_set1.toArray(my_svar);
    for(int k=0;k<my_svar.length();k++){
        System.out.println(my_svar[k]);}
    System.out.println(my_set1);
```

244: What is the purpose of get function in hash table?

Answer:

a) An object containing the value linked with specified key is returned. If the specified key is not present, null object will be returned.

b) Example:

```
    Object get(Object my_key1):
HashTable my_hshtbl = new HashTable();
...
my_hshtbl.get(7);
```

245: How will you add the data into the hash table?

Answer:

a) Data can be added into the hash table using 'put' method

b) Example:

```
HashTable my_hshtbl = new HashTable();
...
my_hshtbl.put(7,9);
```

c) Adds the key and value to the hash table. If the key is present already, the previous value of the key will be returned

246: How will you get the value of the key in property class?

Answer:

a) We can get the value of the key in property class using 'getProperty' method

b) Example:

```
Property my_prop1 =new Property();
```

```
my_prop1.put("ABC", "250");
System.out.println(my_prop1.
getProperty("ABC"));//250
```

c) Returns the values of specified key. If the key is not present in the list, a null object is returned

247: How will you add the text to the list and display the property list?

Answer:

a) Using 'store' function, we can add text to the list and display the property list

b) Example:

```
Property my_prop1 =new Property();
...
my_prop1 .store(OutputStream my_opstrm, "
my_txt1");
```

c) Once specified text is added to the file, the property list will be sent to the outputstream for display

248: Describe about 'pop' and 'peek' function in the stack.

Answer:

Pop function: Returns the top element in the stack and then deletes it.

Peek function: returns the top element without deleting it from the stack.

Example:

```
Stack status;
...
status.peek();
```

```
status.pop();
```

249: How will you add the objects to the collection?

Answer:

a) We can add the objects to the collection using 'add' method

b) Passed object is added to the invoking collection

c) When the object is added successfully, it returns true. Else if the object is present already, returns false

Example:

```
List my_list1 = new ArrayList();
my_list1.add("h");
```

250: How will you insert the elements from one collection into another collection?

Answer:

a) Using 'addAll' function, we can insert the elements from one collection to another

b) Elements in the passed collection are added to the invoked collection

c) Returns true, if insertion is successful. Else returns false

Example:

```
List my_list1 = new ArrayList();
my_list1.add("h");
System.out.println(my_list1); //[ h]
Collections.addAll(my_list1, "e", "l", "o");
System.out.println(my_list1);
```

251: How will you get the iterator for the list?

Answer:

a) **listIterator:** Iterator is returned to the start of the invoking list

b) **listIerator(intmy_indxpsntn):** The invoking list that starts from the specified index receives the Iterator using this function

252: In a collection of elements, after retrieving some elements, how will know still there are elements to retrieve?

Answer:

a) Using 'hasMoreElements' method in enumeration interface

b) Has the return type of 'Boolean'

c) Returns 'true' when there are elements to retrieve, else false

253: What is the purpose of nextElement()?

Answer:

It returns the next object in the list.

Example:

```
Enumeration my_var1;
Vector my_var2= new Vector();
...
my_var1=my_var2.elements();
while( my_var1.hasMoreElements()){
    System.out.println(my_var1.nextElement());}
```

254: What is the purpose of 'retain' function in collection interface?

Answer:

a) The elements in the invoking collection will be removed and it will retain the elements which are in the collection passed as an argument
b) Returns true if the invoking collection is changed, else false
Example:
booleanretainAll(Collection my_colctnname){}

255: What is the difference between 'removeAll' and 'retainAll' functions?

Answer:

a) Both function takes a 'collection' as argument
b) removeAll() removes the elements that are in the collection passed as an argument
c) retainAll() removes the elements that are not in the collection passed as an argument by retaining the other elements

256: Give an example for 'set' interface.

Answer:

```
int my_var1[]={21,31,51,41,81};
Set <integer>my_iset = new HashSet<integer>();
try{
    for(int y=0;y<5;y++){
        my_iset.add(my_var1[y]);
```

```
    }
System.out.println(my_iset);
}
TreeSetmy_sortediset = new TreeSet<integer>(my_iset);
System.out.println(my_Sorted_list);
System.out.println(my_sortediset);
}
```

257: How will you get the elements that are less than a particular element from the collection?

Answer:

a) Using 'headSet'function in Sortedset Interface, we can get the elements that are less than a particular element from the collection

b) Returns the elements that are less than the element passed to this function

c) Example:

```
SortedSet my_sset1 = new SortedSet[];
my_sset1.headSet(7);
```

258: How will you get the elements that are greater than a particular element from the collection?

Answer:

a) Using 'tailSet' function in Sortedset Interface, we can get the elements that are greater than a particular element from the collection

b) Returns the elements that are greater than the element passed to this function

c) Example:

```
SortedSet my_sset1 = new SortedSet[];
my_sset1.tailSet(7);
```

259: How will you get the first and last element from the collection?

Answer:

The first and last element from the collection are obtained using 'first' and 'last'function

Example:

```
int my_var1[]={1,5,3};
Set <integer>my_iset = new HashSet();
for(int y=0;y<3;y++){
my_iset.add(my_var1[y]);}
System.out.println("First element:" + my_iset.first()); // 1
System.out.println("Last element:" + my_iset.last()); //3
```

260: What is the purpose of 'subSet' function in SortedSet Interface?

Answer:

a) It returns the sorted elements.
b) Used to get the subset from the sorted elements .

Example:

```
SortedSetmy_iset = new TreeSet();
my_iset.add(2);
my_iset.add(4);
my_iset.add(1);
my_iset.add(5);
```

```
my_iset.add(3);
Sytem.out.println(iset); // [1,2,3,4,5]
System.out.println(iset.subSet(2,4)); //[2,3,4]
```

261: What are the exceptions thrown by map interface methods?

Answer:

a) **ClassCastException:** Incompatible Objects
b) **NoSuchElementException**: No Items in invoking map
c) **UnSupportedOperationException:** Attempt to change Unmodifiable map
d) **NullPointerException:** Null object

262: How will you replace the particular element in the linkedlist?

Answer:

We can replace the particular element in linkedlist using 'set' function. The arguments of the function are the index of an element to be replaced and the element to be added.

Example:

```
LinkedListmy_lnkdlst= new LinkedList();
...
System.out.println(my_lnkdlst); // [A,B,G,D,E]
my_lnkdlst.set(3, 'C');
System.out.println(my_lnkdlst); //[A,B,C,D,E]
```

263: How will you get the index of the specified element's last occurrence?

Answer:

We can get the index of the specified element's last occurance using 'lastIndexOf()'
An Element is passed as an argument to this function, returns the index of last occurrence of the element.
Example:

```
Int my_var1={1,3,6,8,3,9};
Set my_iset = new Set();
for (int k=0;k<=4;k++){
    my_iset.add(my_var1);}
System.out.println(my_iset); // [1,3,6,8,3,9]
System.out.println(my_iset.lastIndexOf(3)); // 4
```

264: How will you get the index of the specified element's first occurrence?

Answer:

We can get the index of the specified element's first occurance using 'firstIndexOf()'
An Element is passed as an argument to this function, returns the index of first occurrence of the element.
Example:

```
Int my_var1={1,3,6,8,3,9};
Set my_iset = new Set();
for (int k=0;k<=4;k++){
    my_iset.add(my_var1);}
System.out.println(my_iset); // [1,3,6,8,3,9]
System.out.println(my_iset.firstIndexOf(3)); // 1
```

265: How will you get the first and last element from the linkedlist?

Answer:

We can get the first and last element from the linkedlist using 'getFirst' and 'getLast' functions.

getFirst() returns the first element in the linked list.

getLast() returns the last element in the linked list.

Example:

```
LinkedListmy_lnkdlst= new LinkedList();
...
System.out.println(my_lnkdlst); // [1, 2, 4, 5, 6]
System.out.println(my_lnkdlst.getFirst()); // [1]
System.out.println(my_lnkdlst.getLast()); // [6]
```

266: How will you add an element at the first position of the linked list?

Answer:

Using 'addFirst' function, we can add an element at the first position of the linked list.

Element to be added is passed as an argument to the function.

Example:

```
LinkedListmy_lnkdlst= new LinkedList();
...
System.out.println(my_lnkdlst); // [1, 2, 4, 5, 6]
System.out.println(my_lnkdlst.getFirst()); // [1]
System.out.println(my_lnkdlst.addFirst(0));
System.out.println(my_lnkdlst.getFirst()); // [0]
```

267: How will you add the element at the last position of the linked list?

Answer:

Using 'addLast' function, we can add an element at the last position of the linked list.

Element to be added is passed as an argument to the function.

Example:

```
LinkedListmy_lnkdlst= new LinkedList();
...
System.out.println(my_lnkdlst); // [1, 2, 4, 5, 6]
System.out.println(my_lnkdlst.getLast()); // [6]
System.out.println(my_lnkdlst.addLast(7));
System.out.println(my_lnkdlst.getLast()); // [7]
```

268: Compare List<Employee> and List<? Extends Employee>.

Answer:

List<Employee>: Contains instance of type Employee.

List<?extends Employee>: Contains instance of Employee and subclass of Employee.

269: Can you modify a collection if wild card is used as List<?>?

Answer:

No. Data can only be read and inserted into this collection.

270: What will happen if you do not declare arraylist using generics and try to get the values?

Answer:

Type casting will be required. Otherwise compile time error will occur since the arraylist without generics will always be of Object type.

```
List fruitList = new ArrayList();
    fruitList.add("apple");
String myfruit = fruitList.get(0); // Compilation error.
String myfruit = (String) fruitList.get(0);
```

271: How will you iterate over arraylist using advanced for loop?

Answer:

```
List<String>fruitList = new ArrayList<String>();
fruitList.add("apple");
fruitList.add("orange");
fruitList.add("mango");

for (String fruit : fruitList) {
    System.out.println("Fruit : " + fruit);
}
```

272: Can we overload static method in java?

Answer:

a) Yes. Static method can be overloaded but cannot be overridden

b) If static method is overridden, it won't give any compilation error. However value will not change. For instance if you are changing the value of a variable while overridding static method, value will not change. Variable's value of Super class will remain the same

273: Describe the method that provides the interface for database in Java.

Answer:

JDBC(Java Database Connectivity) provides database connection by defining classes and interface. Used for communication between the java application the database. Pl/SQL and SQL can be executed by JDBC and provide access for RDBMS by embedding the sql queries in java code.

274: Describe how database connection is achieved using JDBC.

Answer:

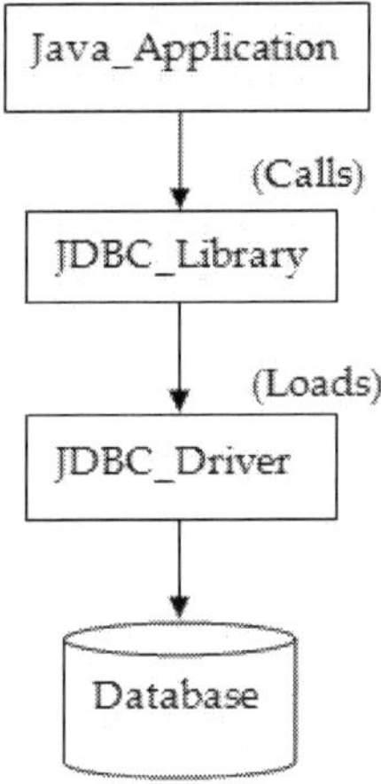

275: Describe the way to load jdbc driver.

Answer:

Jdbc driver is loaded by jdbc library. This will be done by calling the function "Class.forName" with driver class name as argument. An instance of the driver class will be created once the driver is loaded.

Example:

```
try{
    Class.forName("// Driver name");
}
```

276: How will you establish a JDBC connection?

Answer:

We can establish a JDBC connection using 'getConnection'function in the driverclass. It takes three arguments(jdbcurl, user_name, password) to connect the database and returns the connection object. The connection object contains information about database, table and fields.

Example:

```
try{
    Connection
    my_dbconctn=DriverManager.getConnection(my_url,
    "user_name1", "my_pwd");}
```

277: How will you execute the 'SQL' queries?

Answer:

Using 'createStatement' function we can execute SQL queries. Once the connection is established to the database using 'connection'object ,the 'statement' object is instantiated from the connection object using 'createSatement' function.

Example:

```
Connection
my_conn=DriverManager.getConnection(my_url,"shobi",
"shobi");
Statement my_stmtobj = my_conn.createStatement();
```

278: What are the types of statements available in the statement object?

Answer:

a) **Statement:** Simple sql queries that are executed without parameters
b) **Callable:** Executes a call to the function that is stored in the database
c) **Prepared:** Precompiled sql queries are executed with/without parameters

279: How will you execute the precompiled queries?

Answer:

a) Using 'prepared statement' in the statement object
b) Precompiled queries can be executed with/without parameter using this statement
c) Syntax:
   PreparedStatement my_preprdstmt1(String my_sql1) ;
d) Returns the object of the prepared statement and that are the precompiled sql queries

280: How will you call a function in the database?

Answer:

a) Using the 'callable statement' in the statement object
b) Returns the object for the 'callablestatement' and it is the SQL statement calling the procedure in database
c) Syntax:
   CallableStatement my_calblstmt1(String my_sql2)

281: What are the methods provided by the statement interface to interact with database?

Answer:

a) **execute:** for sql queries in String object
b) **executeQuery:** for 'select' statement
c) **executeUpdate:** for creation or modification of tables

282: What is the purpose of ResultSet?

Answer:

When the Statements are executed, the contents of the table are accessed using ResultSet. It retrieves the data in sequential order and points to the data of the current row.

283: What is ResultSetMetaData?

Answer:

a) An interface made from the connection object
b) Contains the details(properties, types, etc) of the column in resultset

284: Can you declare aarraylist as below where generic datatype will differ both left and right side?

Answer:

List<Employee1> myFruitList1 = new ArrayList<String> ();

No. Compile time error will occur. Both should be of same type.

285: How would you know httpsession is removed (when time outs)?

Answer:

The class which needs to be stored in session objects should implement HttpSessionBindingListener interface (javax.servlet.http package) and override valueUnbound() and valueBound() methods. If the session is timed out or removed, the servlet container will invoke the valueUnbound() method on the class object. If this class object is stored into session for the next user valueBound() method will be invoked. HttpSessionBindingListener interfaced is used to track the session events on the particular object.

```
public void
valueBound(HttpSessionBindingEventboundEvent)

public void
valueUnbound(HttpSessionBindingEventunboundEvent)
```

286: How would you set and delete a cookie from the Servlet?

Answer:

Create a cookie and add it in response object. To delete it, set the cookie age as zero using setMaxAge() method and add it in response object.

a) To add a cookie:

```
Cookie cookie = new Cookie("username", "abc");
response.addCookie(cookie);
```

b) To delete a cookie:

```
cookie.setValue("username", null);
cookie.setMaxAge(0);
response.addCookie(cookie);
```

287: How would you invalidate a session if the user closes the browser window?

Answer:

If the client browser gets closed server would not be able to identify it. We can use client side validation to monitor browser window event and report it to servlet to invalidate it. Otherwise session will be invalidated automatically once it is timed out which is configured in the application. So if next request comes from client to server, it will create a new session.

288: What is Server Side push and use of it?

Answer:

If the client requests for data to server, it is called Client pull. i.e) client pulls the data from the server. Sometimes server needs to send the data to client continuously to remain sync between server database and client page. This is called Server side push. E.g. monitor which will display online status such as in railway station, airport, and share market status.

Server keeps pushing the data to server. It is very expensive since the sockets remain open. Server does not open TCP connection every time. When it sends the initial data to client, it will leave the initial connection open and keeps sending the data and client will wait for the next information.

289: What is Client refresh/Client pull mechanism and how do we achieve it?

Answer:

Since server side push is an expensive approach, we can use client refresh mechanism. It will refresh the client browser page automatically for every 3 or 5 seconds which is given as below. For every 3 seconds client will send a request to server for the information and servlet will retrieve it and send it to browser. HTTP-EQUIV attribute information will be added to the http response header.

```
<META HTTP-EQUIV="Refresh" CONTENT="3;
URL=/servlets/testServlet/">
```

290: How would you achieve/make Client Auto Refresh using servlets?

Answer:

Client browser page will be refreshed in every 5 (given) seconds. i.e server will send request to client for every 5 seconds using addHeader() method of response object till the servlet gets destroyed.

```
Public void doGet(HttpServletRequest req,
HttpServletResponseresponse) throws ServletException,
java.io.IOException {
    HttpSession session = req.getSession();
    ...
    response.addHeader("Refresh", "5");
    response.setContentType("text/html"); //If response is text
    message
    ...
}
```

291: What are the options available for deleting session data?

Answer:

a) **Setting the session timeout:** To set the time out for the individual session using setMaxInactiveInterval() method.

This time value is seconds

public void setMaxInactiveInterval(intmaxInterval)

b) **Deleting the entire session:** To delete the entire session using invalidate() method

public void invalidate()

c) **Configure web.xml:** To configure the session time out value in web.xml. This time value is minutes. If this value is retrieved in servlet using getMaxInactiveInterval() method, it will return it in seconds

<session-config>

<session-timeout>5</session-timeout>

</session-config>

d) **Remove particular attribute:** To remove particular attribute or remove the value of particular key using removeAttribute() on session object.

public void removeAttribute(String param1)

e) **Log the user out:** To call logoutServlet to remove the client from the server and invalidate all the users' session

292: What will happen if you call run() method directly rather than calling start()?

Answer:

a) **Start():** Creates new thread and it will call run() implicitly and execute the code inside run() method on a new thread

b) **Run():** Without creating new thread, the code inside run() method will be executed on the same thread

293: What is the difference between synchronized static method

and synchronized non static method?

Answer:

a) Static Synchronized method acquires a lock of the Class object related with the class where the static method is defined

b) Non-static(Instance) Synchronized method acquires a lock of the object through which the method will be invoked

294: Which thread will be started when JVM starts?

Answer:

The thread which executes main() in java will be started first when JVM starts

295: How many locks will be acquired for an object?

Answer:

Only one lock for each object

296: If a current running thread calls a new thread, what is the priority of newly created thread?

Answer:

Equal priority as the current running thread

297: What will happen if you synchronize variables?

Answer:

a) Compile time error. Variables and classes cannot be synchronized

b) Only methods can be synchronized

HR Questions

Review these typical interview questions and think about how you would answer them. Read the answers listed; you will find best possible answers along with strategies and suggestions.

1: Where do you find ideas?

Answer:

Ideas can come from all places, and an interviewer wants to see that your ideas are just as varied. Mention multiple places that you gain ideas from, or settings in which you find yourself brainstorming. Additionally, elaborate on how you record ideas or expand upon them later.

2: How do you achieve creativity in the workplace?

Answer:

It's important to show the interviewer that you're capable of being resourceful and innovative in the workplace, without stepping outside the lines of company values. Explain where ideas normally stem from for you (examples may include an exercise such as list-making or a mind map), and connect this to a particular task in your job that it would be helpful to be creative in.

3: How do you push others to create ideas?

Answer:

If you're in a supervisory position, this may be requiring employees to submit a particular number of ideas, or to complete regular idea-generating exercises, in order to work their creative muscles. However, you can also push others around you to create ideas simply by creating more of your own. Additionally, discuss with the interviewer the importance of questioning people as a way to inspire ideas and change.

4: Describe your creativity.

Answer:

Try to keep this answer within the professional realm, but if you have an impressive background in something creative outside of your employment history, don't be afraid to include it in your answer also. The best answers about creativity will relate problem-solving skills, goal-setting, and finding innovative ways to tackle a project or make a sale in the workplace. However, passions outside of the office are great, too (so long as they don't cut into your work time or mental space).

5: How would you handle a negative coworker?

Answer:

Everyone has to deal with negative coworkers – and the single best way to do so is to remain positive. You may try to build a relationship with the coworker or relate to them in some way, but even if your efforts are met with a cold shoulder, you must retain your positive attitude. Above all, stress that you would never allow a coworker's negativity to impact your own work or productivity.

6: What would you do if you witnessed a coworker surfing the web, reading a book, etc, wasting company time?

Answer:

The interviewer will want to see that you realize how detrimental it is for employees to waste company time, and that it is not something you take lightly. Explain the way you would adhere to company policy, whether that includes talking to the coworker yourself, reporting the behavior straight to a supervisor, or talking to someone in HR.

7: How do you handle competition among yourself and other employees?

Answer:

Healthy competition can be a great thing, and it is best to stay focused on the positive aspects of this here. Don't bring up conflict among yourself and other coworkers, and instead focus on the motivation to keep up with the great work of others, and the ways in which coworkers may be a great support network in helping to push you to new successes.

8: When is it okay to socialize with coworkers?

Answer:

This question has two extreme answers (all the time, or never), and your interviewer, in most cases, will want to see that you fall somewhere in the middle. It's important to establish solid relationships with your coworkers, but never at the expense of getting work done. Ideally, relationship-building can happen with exercises of teamwork and special projects, as well as in the break room.

9: Tell me about a time when a major change was made at your last job, and how you handled it.

Answer:

Provide a set-up for the situation including the old system, what the change was, how it was implemented, and the results of the change, and include how you felt about each step of the way. Be sure that your initial thoughts on the old system are neutral, and that your excitement level grows with each step of the new change, as an interviewer will be pleased to see your adaptability.

10: When delegating tasks, how do you choose which tasks go to which team members?

Answer:

The interviewer is looking to gain insight into your thought process with this question, so be sure to offer thorough reasoning behind your choice. Explain that you delegate tasks based on each individual's personal strengths, or that you look at how many other projects each person is working on at the time, in order to create the best fit possible.

11: Tell me about a time when you had to stand up for something you believed strongly about to coworkers or a supervisor.

Answer:

While it may be difficult to explain a situation of conflict to an interviewer, this is a great opportunity to display your passions and convictions, and your dedication to your beliefs. Explain not just the situation to the interviewer, but also elaborate on why it was so important to you to stand up for the issue, and how your coworker or supervisor responded to you afterward – were they more respectful? Unreceptive? Open-minded? Apologetic?

12: Tell me about a time when you helped someone finish their

work, even though it wasn't "your job."

Answer:

Though you may be frustrated when required to pick up someone else's slack, it's important that you remain positive about lending a hand. The interviewer will be looking to see if you're a team player, and by helping someone else finish a task that he or she couldn't manage alone, you show both your willingness to help the team succeed, and your own competence.

13: What are the challenges of working on a team? How do you handle this?

Answer:

There are many obvious challenges to working on a team, such as handling different perspectives, navigating individual schedules, or accommodating difficult workers. It's best to focus on one challenge, such as individual team members missing deadlines or failing to keep commitments, and then offer a solution that clearly addresses the problem. For example, you could organize weekly status meetings for your team to discuss progress, or assign shorter deadlines in order to keep the long-term deadline on schedule.

14: Do you value diversity in the workplace?

Answer:

Diversity is important in the workplace in order to foster an environment that is accepting, equalizing, and full of different perspectives and backgrounds. Be sure to show your awareness of these issues, and stress the importance of learning from others' experiences.

15: How would you handle a situation in which a coworker was not accepting of someone else's diversity?

Answer:

Explain that it is important to adhere to company policies regarding diversity, and that you would talk to the relevant supervisors or management team. When it is appropriate, it could also be best to talk to the coworker in question about the benefits of alternate perspectives – if you can handle the situation yourself, it's best not to bring resolvable issues to management.

16: Are you rewarded more from working on a team, or accomplishing a task on your own?

Answer:

It's best to show a balance between these two aspects – your employer wants to see that you're comfortable working on your own, and that you can complete tasks efficiently and well without assistance. However, it's also important for your employer to see that you can be a team player, and that you understand the value that multiple perspectives and efforts can bring to a project.

17: Tell me about a time when you worked additional hours to finish a project.

Answer:

It's important for your employer to see that you are dedicated to your work, and willing to put in extra hours when required or when a job calls for it. However, be careful when explaining why you were called to work additional hours – for instance, did you have to stay late because you set goals poorly earlier in the process? Or on a more positive note, were you working additional hours because a client requested for a deadline to be moved up on short notice? Stress your competence and willingness to give 110% every time.

18: Tell me about a time when your performance exceeded the duties and requirements of your job.

Answer:

If you're a great candidate for the position, this should be an easy question to answer – choose a time when you truly went above and beyond the call of duty, and put in additional work or voluntarily took on new responsibilities. Remain humble, and express gratitude for the learning opportunity, as well as confidence in your ability to give a repeat performance.

19: What is your driving attitude about work?

Answer:

There are many possible good answers to this question, and the interviewer primarily wants to see that you have a great passion for the job and that you will remain motivated in your career if hired. Some specific driving forces behind your success may include hard work, opportunity, growth potential, or success.

20: Do you take work home with you?

Answer:

It is important to first clarify that you are always willing to take work home when necessary, but you want to emphasize as well that it has not been an issue for you in the past. Highlight skills such as time management, goal-setting, and multi-tasking, which can all ensure that work is completed at work.

21: Describe a typical work day to me.

Answer:

There are several important components in your typical work day, and an interviewer may derive meaning from any or all of them, as well as from your ability to systematically lead him or her through the day. Start at the beginning of your day and proceed chronologically, making sure to emphasize steady productivity, time for review, goal-setting, and prioritizing, as well as some additional time to account for unexpected things that may arise.

22: Tell me about a time when you went out of your way at your previous job.

Answer:

Here it is best to use a specific example of the situation that required you to go out of your way, what your specific position would have required that you did, and how you went above that. Use concrete details, and be sure to include the results, as well as reflection on what you learned in the process.

23: Are you open to receiving feedback and criticisms on your job performance, and adjusting as necessary?

Answer:

This question has a pretty clear answer – yes – but you'll need to display a knowledge as to why this is important. Receiving feedback and criticism is one thing, but the most important part of that process is to then implement it into your daily work. Keep a good attitude, and express that you always appreciate constructive feedback.

24: What inspires you?

Answer:

You may find inspiration in nature, reading success stories, or mastering a difficult task, but it's important that your inspiration is positively-based and that you're able to listen and tune into it when it appears. Keep this answer generally based in the professional world, but where applicable, it may stretch a bit into creative exercises in your personal life that, in turn, help you in achieving career objectives.

25: How do you inspire others?

Answer:

This may be a difficult question, as it is often hard to discern the effects of inspiration in others. Instead of offering a specific example of a time when you inspired someone, focus on general principles such as leading by example that you employ in your professional life. If possible, relate this to a quality that someone who inspired you possessed, and discuss the way you have modified or modeled it in your own work.

26: Ten years ago, what were your career goals?

Answer:

In reflecting back to what your career goals were ten years ago, it's important to show the ways in which you've made progress in that time. Draw distinct links between specific objectives that you've achieved, and speak candidly about how it felt to reach those goals. Remain positive, upbeat, and growth-oriented, even if you haven't yet achieved all of the goals you set out to reach.

27: Tell me about a weakness you used to have, and how you changed it.

Answer:

Choose a non-professional weakness that you used to have, and outline the process you went through in order to grow past it. Explain the weakness itself, why it was problematic, the action steps you planned, how you achieved them, and the end result.

28: Tell me about your goal-setting process.

Answer:

When describing your goal-setting process, clearly outline the way that you create an outline for yourself. It may be helpful to offer an example of a particular goal you've set in the past, and use this as a starting point to guide the way you created action steps, check-in points, and how the goal was eventually achieved.

29: Tell me about a time when you solved a problem by creating actionable steps to follow.

Answer:

This question will help the interviewer to see how you talented you are in outlining, problem resolution, and goal-setting.

Explain thoroughly the procedure of outlining the problem, establishing steps to take, and then how you followed the steps (such as through check-in points along the way, or intermediary goals).

30: Where do you see yourself five years from now?

Answer:

Have some idea of where you would like to have advanced to in the position you're applying for, over the next several years. Make sure that your future plans line up with you still working for the company, and stay positive about potential advancement. Focus on future opportunities, and what you're looking forward to – but make sure your reasons for advancement are admirable, such as greater experience and the chance to learn, rather than simply being out for a higher salary.

31: When in a position, do you look for opportunities to promote?

Answer:

There's a fine balance in this question – you want to show the interviewer that you have initiative and motivation to advance in your career, but not at the expense of appearing opportunistic or selfishly-motivated. Explain that you are always open to growth opportunities, and very willing to take on new responsibilities as your career advances.

32: On a scale of 1 to 10, how successful has your life been?

Answer:

Though you may still have a long list of goals to achieve, it's important to keep this answer positively-focused. Choose a high number between 7 and 9, and explain that you feel your life has been largely successful and satisfactory as a result of several specific achievements or experiences. Don't go as high as a 10, as the interviewer may not believe your response or in your ability to reason critically.

33: What is your greatest goal in life?

Answer:

It's okay for this answer to stray a bit into your personal life, but best if you can keep it professionally-focused. While specific goals are great, if your personal goal doesn't match up exactly with one of the company's objectives, you're better off keeping your goal a little more generic and encompassing, such as "success in my career" or "leading a happy and fulfilling life." Keep your answer brief, and show a decisive nature – most importantly, make it clear that you've already thought about this question and know what you want.

34: Tell me about a time when you set a goal in your personal life and achieved it.

Answer:

The interviewer can see that you excel at setting goals in your professional life, but he or she also wants to know that you are consistent in your life and capable of setting goals outside of the office as well. Use an example such as making a goal to eat more healthily or to drink more water, and discuss what steps you outlined to achieve your goal, the process of taking action, and the final results as well.

35: What is your greatest goal in your career?

Answer:

Have a very specific goal of something you want to achieve in your career in mind, and be sure that it's something the position clearly puts you in line to accomplish. Offer the goal as well as your plans to get there, and emphasize clear ways in which this position will be an opportunity to work toward the goal.

36: Tell me about a time when you achieved a goal.

Answer:

Start out with how you set the goal, and why you chose it. Then, take the interviewer through the process of outlining the goal, taking steps to achieve it, the outcome, and finally, how you felt after achieving it or recognition you received. The most important part of this question includes the planning and implementation of strategies, so focus most of your time on explaining these aspects. However, the preliminary decisions and end results are also important, so make sure to include them as well.

37: What areas of your work would you still like to improve in? What are your plans to do this?

Answer:

While you may not want the interviewer to focus on things you could improve on, it's important to be self-aware of your own growth opportunities. More importantly, you can impress an interviewer by having specific goals and actions outlined in order to facilitate your growth, even if your area of improvement is something as simple as increasing sales or finding new ways to create greater efficiency.

38: What is customer service?

Answer:

Customer service can be many things – and the most important consideration in this question is that you have a creative answer. Demonstrate your ability to think outside the box by offering a confident answer that goes past a basic definition, and that shows you have truly considered your own individual view of what it means to take care of your customers. The thoughtful consideration you hold for customers will speak for itself.

39: Tell me about a time when you went out of your way for a customer.

Answer:

It's important that you offer an example of a time you truly went out of your way – be careful not to confuse something that felt like a big effort on your part, with something your employer would expect you to do anyway. Offer an example of the customer's problems, what you did to solve it, and the way the customer responded after you took care of the situation.

40: How do you gain confidence from customers?

Answer:

This is a very open-ended question that allows you to show your customer service skills to the interviewer. There are many possible answers, and it is best to choose something that you've had great experience with, such as "by handling situations with transparency," "offering rewards," or "focusing on great communication." Offer specific examples of successes you've had.

41: Tell me about a time when a customer was upset or agitated – how did you handle the situation?

Answer:

Similarly to handling a dispute with another employee, the most important part to answering this question is to first set up the scenario, offer a step-by-step guide to your particular conflict resolution style, and end by describing the way the conflict was resolved. Be sure that in answering questions about your own conflict resolution style, that you emphasize the importance of open communication and understanding from both parties, as well as a willingness to reach a compromise or other solution.

42: When can you make an exception for a customer?

Answer:

Exceptions for customers can generally be made when in accordance with company policy or when directed by a supervisor. Display an understanding of the types of situations in which an exception should be considered, such as when a customer has endured a particular hardship, had a complication with an order, or at a request.

43: What would you do in a situation where you were needed by

both a customer and your boss?

Answer:

While both your customer and your boss have different needs of you and are very important to your success as a worker, it is always best to try to attend to your customer first – however, the key is explaining to your boss why you are needed urgently by the customer, and then to assure your boss that you will attend to his or her needs as soon as possible (unless it's absolutely an urgent matter).

44: What is the most important aspect of customer service?

Answer:

While many people would simply state that customer satisfaction is the most important aspect of customer service, it's important to be able to elaborate on other important techniques in customer service situations. Explain why customer service is such a key part of business, and be sure to expand on the aspect that you deem to be the most important in a way that is reasoned and well-thought out.

45: Is it best to create low or high expectations for a customer?

Answer:

You may answer this question either way (after, of course, determining that the company does not have a clear opinion on the matter). However, no matter which way you answer the question, you must display a thorough thought process, and very clear reasoning for the option you chose. Offer pros and cons of each, and include the ultimate point that tips the scale in favor of your chosen answer.

46: Why did you choose your college major?

Answer:

It's important to display interest in your work, and if your major is related to your current field, it will be simple for you to relate the two. Perhaps you even knew while in college that you wanted to do a job similar to this position, and so you chose the major so as to receive the education and training you needed to succeed. If your major doesn't relate clearly, it's still important to express a sense of passion for your choice, and to specify the importance of pursuing something that matters to you – which is how you made the decision to come to your current career field instead.

47: Tell me about your college experience.

Answer:

It's best to keep this answer positive – don't focus on parties, pizza, or procrastinating. Instead, offer a general summary of the benefits you received in college, followed by an anecdote of a favorite professor or course that opened up your way of thinking about the field you're in. This is a great opportunity for you to show your passion for your career, make sure to answer enthusiastically and confidently.

48: What is the most unique thing about yourself that you would bring to this position?

Answer:

This question is often asked as a close to an interview, and it gives you a final chance to highlight your best qualities to the employer. Treat the question like a sort of review, and explain why your specific mix of education, experience, and passions will be the ideal combination for the employer. Remain confident but humble, and keep your answer to about two minutes.

49: How did your last job stand up to your previous expectations of it?

Answer:

While it's okay to discuss what you learned if you expected too much out of a previous job, it's best to keep this question away from negative statements or portrayals. Focus your answer around what your previous job did hold that you had expected, and how much you enjoyed those aspects of the position.

50: How did you become interested in this field?

Answer:

This is the chance for you to show your passion for your career – and the interviewer will be assured that you are a great candidate if it's obvious that you enjoy your job. You can include a brief anecdote here in order to make your interest personal, but be sure that it is *brief*. Offer specific names of mentors or professors who aided in your discovery, and make it clear that you love what you do.

51: What was the greatest thing you learned while in school?

Answer:

By offering a lesson you learned outside of the classroom, you can show the interviewer your capacity for creativity, learning, and reflection. The practical lessons you learned in the classroom are certainly invaluable in their own right and may pertain closely to the position, but showing the mastery of a concept that you had to learn on your own will highlight your growth potential.

52: Tell me about a time when you had to learn a different skill set for a new position.

Answer:

Use a specific example to describe what you had to learn and how you set about outlining goals and tasks for yourself. It's important to show that you mastered the skill largely from your dedication to learning it, and because of the systematic approach you took to developing and honing your individual education. Additionally, draw connections between the skill you learned and the new position, and show how well prepared you are for the job.

53: Tell me about a person who has been a great influence in your career.

Answer:

It's important to make this answer easy to relate to – your story should remind the interviewer of the person who was most influential in his or her own career. Explain what you learned from this person and why they inspired you, and how you hope to model them later in your career with future successes.

54: What would this person tell me about you?

Answer:

Most importantly, if this person is one of your references –they had better know who you are! There are all too many horror stories of professors or past employers being called for a reference, and not being able to recall when they knew you or why you were remarkable, which doesn't send a very positive message to potential employers. This person should remember you as being enthusiastic, passionate, and motivated to learn and succeed.

55: What is the most productive time of day for you?

Answer:

This is a trick question – you should be equally productive all day! While it's normal to become extra motivated for certain projects, and also true that some tasks will require additional work, be sure to emphasize to the interviewer that working diligently throughout the entirety of the day comes naturally to you.

56: What was the most responsibility you were given at your previous job?

Answer:

This question provides you with an opportunity to elaborate on responsibilities that may or may not be on your resume. For instance, your resume may not have allowed room to discuss individual projects you worked on that were really outside the scope of your job responsibilities, but you can tell the interviewer here about the additional work you did and how it translated into new skills and a richer career experience for you.

57: Do you believe you were compensated fairly at your last job?

Answer:

Remember to stay positive, and to avoid making negative comments about your previous employer. If you were not compensated fairly, simply state that you believe your qualities and experience were outside the compensation limitations of the old job, and that you're looking forward to an opportunity that is more in line with the place you're at in your career.

58: Tell me about a time when you received feedback on your work, and enacted it.

Answer:

Try to give an example of feedback your received early in your career, and the steps you took to incorporate it with your work. The most important part of this question is to display the way you learned from the feedback, as well as your willingness to accept suggestions from your superiors. Be sure to offer reflection and understanding of how the feedback helped your work to improve.

59: Tell me about a time when you received feedback on your work that you did not agree with, or thought was unfair. How did you handle it?

Answer:

When explaining that you did not agree with particular feedback or felt it was unfair, you'll need to justify tactfully why the feedback was inaccurate. Then, explain how you communicated directly with the person who offered the feedback, and, most importantly, how you listened to their response, analyzed it, and then came to a mutual agreement.

60: What was your favorite job, and why?

Answer:

It's best if your favorite job relates to the position you're currently applying for, as you can then easily draw connections between why you enjoyed that job and why you are interested in the current position. Additionally, it is extremely important to explain why you've qualified the particular job as your favorite, and what aspects of it you would look for in another job, so that the interviewer can determine whether or not you are a good fit.

61: Tell me about an opportunity that your last position did not allow you to achieve.

Answer:

Stay focused on the positive, and be understanding of the limitations of your previous position. Give a specific example of a goal or career objective that you were not able to achieve, but rather than expressing disappointment over the missed opportunity, discuss the ways you're looking forward to the chance to grow in a new position.

62: Tell me about the worst boss you ever had.

Answer:

It's important to keep this answer brief, and positively focused. While you may offer a couple of short, critical assessments of your boss, focus on the things you learned from working with such an individual, and remain sympathetic to challenges the boss may have faced.

63: What is the best way for a company to advertise?

Answer:

If you're going for a position in any career other than marketing, this question is probably intended to demonstrate your ability to think critically and to provide reflective support for your answers. As such, the particular method you choose is not so important as why you've chosen it. For example, word of mouth advertising is important because customers will inherently trust the source, and social media advertising is important as it reaches new customers quickly and cheaply.

64: Is it better to gain a new customer or to keep an old one?

Answer:

In almost every case, it is better to keep an old customer, and it's important that you are able to articulate why this is. First, new customers generally cost companies more than retaining old ones does, and new customers are more likely to switch to a different company. Additionally, keeping old customers is a great way to provide a stable backbone for the company, as well as to also gain new customers as they are likely to recommend your company to friends.

65: What is the best way to win clients from competitors?

Answer:

There are many schools of thought on the best way to win clients from competitors, and unless you know that your interviewer adheres to a specific thought or practice, it's best to keep this question general. Rather than using absolute language, focus on the benefits of one or two strategies and show a clear, critical understanding of how these ways can succeed in a practical application.

66: How do you feel about companies monitoring internet usage?

Answer:

Generally speaking, most companies will monitor some degree of internet usage over their employees – and during an interview is not the best time to rebel against this practice. Instead, focus on positive aspects such as the way it can lead to increased productivity for some employees who may be easily lost in the world of resourceful information available to them.

67: What is your first impression of our company?

Answer:

Obviously, this should be a positive answer! Pick out a couple key components of the company's message or goals that you especially identify with or that pertain to your experience, and discuss why you believe these missions are so important.

68: Tell me about your personal philosophy on business.

Answer:

Your personal philosophy on business should be well-thought out, and in line with the missions and objectives of the company. Stay focused on positive aspects such as the service it can provide, and the lessons people gain in business, and offer insight as to where your philosophy has come from.

69: What's most important in a business model: sales, customer service, marketing, management, etc.?

Answer:

For many positions, it may be a good strategy to tailor this answer to the type of field you're working in, and to explain why that aspect of business is key. However, by explaining that each aspect is integral to the function as a whole, you can display a greater sense of business savvy to the interviewer and may stand out in his or her mind as a particularly aware candidate.

70: How do you keep up with news and emerging trends in the field?

Answer:

The interviewer wants to see that you are aware of what's currently going on in your field. It is important that your education does not stop after college, and the most successful candidates will have a list of resources they regularly turn to already in place, so that they may stay aware and engaged in developing trends.

71: Would you have a problem adhering to company policies on social media?

Answer:

Social media concerns in the workplace have become a greater issue, and many companies now outline policies for the use of social media. Interviewers will want to be assured that you won't have a problem adhering to company standards, and that you will maintain a consistent, professional image both in the office and online.

72: Tell me about one of the greatest problems facing *X industry* today.

Answer:

If you're involved in your career field, and spend time on your own studying trends and new developments, you should be able to display an awareness of both problems and potential solutions coming up in the industry. Research some of the latest news before heading into the interview, and be prepared to discuss current events thoroughly.

73: What do you think it takes to be successful in our company?

Answer:

Research the company prior to the interview. Be aware of the company's mission and main objectives, as well as some of the biggest names in the company, and also keep in mind how they achieved success. Keep your answer focused on specific objectives you could reach in order to help the company achieve its goals.

74: What is your favorite part of working in this career field?

Answer:

This question is an opportunity to discuss some of your favorite aspects of the job, and to highlight why you are a great candidate for the particular position. Choose elements of the work you enjoy that are related to what you would do if hired for the position. Remember to remain enthusiastic and excited for the opportunities you could attain in the job.

75: What do you see happening to your career in the next 10 years?

Answer:

If you're plugged in to what's happening in your career now, and are making an effort to stay abreast of emerging trends in your field, you should be able to offer the interviewer several predictions as to where your career or field may be heading. This insight and level of awareness shows a level of dedication and interest that is important to employers.

INDEX

Advanced Java Interview Questions

Object Serialization

17: What methods are there in Serializable interface?

18: In which scenarios serialization should be used?

19: What can be the cause of NotSerializableException during object serialization?

20: Which methods can be overridden to change default serialization behavior in order to control complex object serialization process?

21: Which interface is to be implemented if we want to have complete control over your class's serialization process?

22: Name the methods that are to be overridden when Externalizable is implemented.

23: Consider the following scenario:

24: Is it correct to say that when an object is de-serialized, its constructor is called?

25: I have a class called Student that is Serializable. It has an instance variable of type String called 'name'. Since 'name' is not of primitive type, should we expect serialization failure?

26: Are all primitive wrapper classes Serializable?

27: Assume you have a Serializable class where its super class does not implement Serializable interface. The super class defines a no- argument constructor and a String argument constructor. Which constructor of the super class will get called during de-serialization?

28: Consider the following scenario:

Generics

29: Explain Java Generics.

30: Write a program to explain Generic Methods.

31: Differentiate between List<? extends T> and List <? super T>

32: Explain the following code:

33: Explain the Type Parameters in Generics.

34: How to avoid casting when retrieving elements from a collection?

35: Review the following code. Will it compile? Will it run?

36: Can you use more than one parameterized type in a declaration? Give an example.

37: How can you declare a generic method using a type say: T, which is not defined in the class?

38: Can you instantiate an array of a generic type?

CORBA

39: Explain CORBA and how it serves Java.

40: Explain the Life Cycle of CORBA application.

41: Explain CORBAservices and CORBAfacilities.

42: Explain how objects are passed in CORBA.

43: Which operation invocation techniques are provided by CORBA 2.0?

44: What is Synchronous operation invocation technique?

45: What is the Deferred Synchronous operation invocation technique?

46: What is the One-way operation invocation technique?

47: How are the services offered by distributed object defined?

48: Which CORBA service defines how objects are copied, moved, created and removed?

49: Name the CORBA service that decouples the communication between distributed objects.

50: Does an object interface represent how it is or will be implemented?

51: Is it correct to say that IDL provides object's implementation?

52: Name the programming languages for which OMG has standardized on language bindings.

53: Name the IDL basic data types.

54: You want to use constructed data types in IDL. What choices do you have?

55: Which compiler is used to compile IDL declarations?

56: What is used by the client to issue a request on a CORBA object?

57: IDL construct 'module' corresponds to which Java construct?

58: IDL construct 'operation' corresponds to which Java construct?

59: Which fundamental mechanisms are available to obtain object references?

Threading

60: Explain the different stages of a thread.

61: Explain the output of the following program.

62: Does the following code indicate a safe thread implementation?

63: We know what a Deadlock is. Explain Livelock.

64: Explain with example how to create a thread.

65: Explain wait(), yield() and sleep() methods in Java.

66: There are three threads Thread1, Thread2 and Thread3? How do you ensure sequence Thread1, Thread2, Thread3 in Java?

67: What are the two ways of creating Threads in Java?

68: What happens if start() is called more than once on same thread object?

69: Can you create more than one Thread objects using the same Runnable object as the target?

70: When does a thread object become a thread of execution?

71: When is a thread considered alive?

72: A new thread is started. In which state it will enter?

73: When does a thread enter into the dead state?

74: You have a single-processor machine. How many threads can be made running at a time?

75: Does the order in which threads were started determine the order in which they'll run?

76: Do threads take turns in any fair way?

77: How can you guarantee that your threads will take turns regardless of the underlying JVM?

78: You invoked sleep() method on your thread to delay its exception for some time. Will it start running as soon as the sleep period is over?

79: What is thread priority and how can you define it?

Servlet

103: In which scenario doPost() is to be used?
104: When comparing doGet with doPost, which one is faster?
105: What is the data limitation of GET request?
106: Name the phases of Servlet life cycle.
107: Can you call doPost manually from a doGet method?
108: Why should I not override the service() method in my HttpServlet?
109: Which one is faster? forward() or sendRedirect() ?
110: sendRedirect() is a two phase process, which are those phases?
111: Why is original request context retained in forward()?
112: You want to redirect a request to another resource that is in the some other domain. Will you use forward()?
113: Where does Servlet run?
114: Which protocols are supported by Java Servlet?
115: How session tracking is done by Servlet container?
116: Define session mapping.
117: Define Servlet context.
118: I want to initialize Servlet using constructor instead of init(). Will I have access to ServletConfig to ServletContext?
119: How do you get the current Servlet path i.e. its location on file system?
120: When does init() method gets called?
121: How to make init() method thread safe?
122: How can you call a Servlet from another Servlet?
123: Give an example to show how RequestDispatcher can be used to forward a request from one Servlet to another.
124: What is the difference between request.getParameter() and request.getAttribute() where request is an instance of
125: How can you access client's directory structure from a Servlet?
126: What are Generic Servlets?
127: What is the difference between Generic and HttpServlet Servlet?
128: Is HttpServlet a concrete class?

129: Since HttpServlet is an Abstract class, which methods it must override?

130: Who controls the life cycle of a Servlet?

131: When a request is mapped to a Servlet, what does the container do?

132: Which method is invoked by the container once it needs to remove the Servlet?

133: What is the purpose of service method?

134: You want to write a Servlet for Http protocol. Which class you need to extend?

135: Which exceptions are thrown by the doXXX methods?

136: Where you can define Servlet mapping?

137: How can you define context init parameter in web.xml?

138: How can you retrieve context init parameters in Servlet?

139: How can you set error page in web.xml?

140: Give an example of Servlet mapping in web.xml.

141: Define ServletContext.

142: Will all the Servlets in a web application share the same ServletConfig?

143: What methods are provided by ServletContextListener interface?

144: When does ServletContextListener gets notified?

145: How to configure ServletContextListener in web.xml?

146: When deploying Servlet on a web container, what is the purpose of WEB-INF?

147: What will happen if I want to use the Servlet 2.1 API instead of Servlet2.0 API?

148: What is lazy loading in servlet?

149: How will you call a servlet along with the parameters in the URL?

Collections

150: Differentiate between Hashtable and Hashmap.

151: Explain how Hashmap works in Java.

152: Differentiate between Comparable and Comparator.
153: Explain the output of the program.
154: Differentiate – Iterator, ListIterator and Enumerator.
155: Both ArrayList and LinkedList implements get(int) method to fetch an object at specified position in list. Which one is faster?
156: Why adding elements to ArrayList can be slow?
157: You want to add an element in the middle of a List. Which List implementation gives you better performance? LinkedList or ArrayList?
158: You want a List whose size will grow with time. You may also need to add elements in between existing elements but you will very seldom need random access. Which List implementation you will prefer?
159: Hashtable defines the following constructor: Hashtable(int initialCapacity, float loadFactor) What is initialCapacity and loadFactor here?
160: What is the Hashtable default load factor?
161: What will be the initial capacity of Hashtable if it is created using: public Hashtable()
162: What is the difference between Hashtable and HashMap?
163: You use the following to get an Object from a HashMap.
164: You have a HashMap and want to get a collection view of the mappings contained in this map? Which method will you invoke?
165: Is Map a Collection?
166: What happens if you try to add a duplicate key in a Map?
167: Which Map implementation will you use if you need to insert, delete, and locate elements in a Map?
168: In which case will you prefer TreeMap over HashMap?
169: How can you tune HashMap and TreeMap?
170: You want to create a single element set using Collection class. How you will do it in a single line of code?
171: What happens if hash value of the key in the map collides with an existing key in the Map?
172: What are the two ways to traverse a collection?

192: Apart from inherited operations from Collection interface, what additional operations are provided by List?
193: Name few of the algorithms supported my List.
194: There are two forms of Queue methods depending on the operation failure. Name them.
195: What are bounded queues?
196: Which Java package contains bounded queues and which one contains un-bounded queues?
197: You have an empty Queue and you try to remove an element using poll(). What will be the result?
198: What will be the outcome of remove() operation conducted on an empty Queue?
199: You want to get the head element of a Queue. What methods can you use?
200: What is the difference between element() and peek() methods of Queue?
201: Name the Queue implementations that allow insertion of null elements.
202: Do Queue implementations generally define element-based versions of the equals and hashCode methods?
203: In concurrent programming, blocking queue methods are required. Does Queue interface provide that?
204: Name the general-purpose Map implementations.
205: When comparing Map with Hashtable, which one of these provides the functionality to remove entries in the midst of iteration?
206: How do you differentiate between Vector and ArrayList?
207: What is the difference between Collection and Collections?
208: Define the java.util.Vector class.
209: What is an Iterator interface?
210: Event handling is supported by which java.util classes and interfaces?
211: What is the java.util.Map?

Design Patterns

Data Structures

234: How will you clear the bits in the BitSet?

235: What is the purpose of the functions "clone" and "equals"?

236: Describe the "flip" function in the bitset.

237: How will you get the current state and hash code for the bit?

238: How will you get the string equivalent and size for the invoking bitset object?

239: How will you add an element to the vector?

240: How will you copy the component of a vector to an array?

241: What is the purpose of ensureCapacity function in vector?

242: Describe about remove and removeAll function.

243: Give an example for 'toArray' function.

244: What is the purpose of get function in hash table?

245: How will you add the data into the hash table?

246: How will you get the value of the key in property class?

247: How will you add the text to the list and display the property list?

248: Describe about 'pop' and 'peek' function in the stack.

249: How will you add the objects to the collection?

250: How will you insert the elements from one collection into another collection?

251: How will you get the iterator for the list?

252: In a collection of elements, after retrieving some elements, how will know still there are elements to retrieve?

253: What is the purpose of nextElement()?

254: What is the purpose of 'retain' function in collection interface?

255: What is the difference between 'removeAll' and 'retainAll' functions?

256: Give an example for 'set' interface.

257: How will you get the elements that are less than a particular element from the collection?

258: How will you get the elements that are greater than a particular element from the collection?

259: How will you get the first and last element from the collection?

260: What is the purpose of 'subSet' function in SortedSet Interface?

287: How would you invalidate a session if the user closes the browser window?

288: What is Server Side push and use of it?

289: What is Client refresh/Client pull mechanism and how do we achieve it?

290: How would you achieve/make Client Auto Refresh using servlets?

291: What are the options available for deleting session data?

292: What will happen if you call run() method directly rather than calling start()?

293: What is the difference between synchronized static method and synchronized non static method?

294: Which thread will be started when JVM starts?

295: How many locks will be acquired for an object?

296: If a current running thread calls a new thread, what is the priority of newly created thread?

297: What will happen if you synchronize variables?

HR Questions

21: Describe a typical work day to me.

22: Tell me about a time when you went out of your way at your previous job.

23: Are you open to receiving feedback and criticisms on your job performance, and adjusting as necessary?

24: What inspires you?

25: How do you inspire others?

26: Ten years ago, what were your career goals?

27: Tell me about a weakness you used to have, and how you changed it.

28: Tell me about your goal-setting process.

29: Tell me about a time when you solved a problem by creating actionable steps to follow.

30: Where do you see yourself five years from now?

31: When in a position, do you look for opportunities to promote?

32: On a scale of 1 to 10, how successful has your life been?

33: What is your greatest goal in life?

34: Tell me about a time when you set a goal in your personal life and achieved it.

35: What is your greatest goal in your career?

36: Tell me about a time when you achieved a goal.

37: What areas of your work would you still like to improve in? What are your plans to do this?

38: What is customer service?

39: Tell me about a time when you went out of your way for a customer.

40: How do you gain confidence from customers?

41: Tell me about a time when a customer was upset or agitated – how did you handle the situation?

42: When can you make an exception for a customer?

43: What would you do in a situation where you were needed by both a customer and your boss?

44: What is the most important aspect of customer service?

45: Is it best to create low or high expectations for a customer?

71: Would you have a problem adhering to company policies on social media?

72: Tell me about one of the greatest problems facing X industry today.

73: What do you think it takes to be successful in our company?

74: What is your favorite part of working in this career field?

75: What do you see happening to your career in the next 10 years?

Some of the following titles might also be handy:

51. Microsoft Access Interview Questions You'll Most Likely Be Asked
52. Microsoft Excel Interview Questions You'll Most Likely Be Asked
53. Microsoft Powerpoint Interview Questions You'll Most Likely Be Asked
54. Microsoft Word Interview Questions You'll Most Likely Be Asked
55. MySQL Interview Questions You'll Most Likely Be Asked
56. NetSuite Interview Questions You'll Most Likely Be Asked
57. Networking Interview Questions You'll Most Likely Be Asked
58. OOPS Interview Questions You'll Most Likely Be Asked
59. Operating Systems Interview Questions You'll Most Likely Be Asked
60. Oracle DBA Interview Questions You'll Most Likely Be Asked
61. Oracle E-Business Suite Interview Questions You'll Most Likely Be Asked
62. ORACLE PL/SQL Interview Questions You'll Most Likely Be Asked
63. Perl Programming Interview Questions You'll Most Likely Be Asked
64. PHP Interview Questions You'll Most Likely Be Asked
65. PMP Interview Questions You'll Most Likely Be Asked
66. Python Interview Questions You'll Most Likely Be Asked
67. RESTful JAVA Web Services Interview Questions You'll Most Likely Be Asked
68. Ruby Interview Questions You'll Most Likely Be Asked
69. Ruby on Rails Interview Questions You'll Most Likely Be Asked
70. SAP ABAP Interview Questions You'll Most Likely Be Asked
71. SAP HANA Interview Questions You'll Most Likely Be Asked
72. SAS Programming Guidelines Interview Questions You'll Most Likely Be Asked
73. Selenium Testing Tools Interview Questions You'll Most Likely Be Asked
74. Silverlight Interview Questions You'll Most Likely Be Asked
75. Software Repositories Interview Questions You'll Most Likely Be Asked
76. Software Testing Interview Questions You'll Most Likely Be Asked
77. SQL Server Interview Questions You'll Most Likely Be Asked
78. Tomcat Interview Questions You'll Most Likely Be Asked
79. UML Interview Questions You'll Most Likely Be Asked
80. Unix Interview Questions You'll Most Likely Be Asked
81. UNIX Shell Programming Interview Questions You'll Most Likely Be Asked
82. VB.NET Interview Questions You'll Most Likely Be Asked
83. Windows Server 2008 R2 Interview Questions You'll Most Likely Be Asked
84. XLXP, XSLT, XPATH, XFORMS & XQuery Interview Questions You'll Most Likely Be Asked
85. XML Interview Questions You'll Most Likely Be Asked

Made in the USA
San Bernardino, CA
18 April 2020

67902704R00093